Managing 00

Surviving the Year 2000 Computing Crisis

Peter de Jager
Richard Bergeon

WILEY COMPUTER PUBLISHING

John Wiley & Sons, Inc.

New York • Chichester • Weinheim •
Brisbane • Singapore • Toronto

Publisher: Katherine Schowalter
Editor: Marjorie Spencer
Managing Editor: Frank Grazioli
Text Design & Composition: North Market Street Graphics, Lancaster, PA

Library of Congress Cataloging-in-Publication Data:

ISBN: 0-471-17937-X
Printed in the United States of America
10 9 8 7 6 5 4 3

Contents

Houston, We Have a Problem

It's New Year's Day 2000 and you're headed to your best friend's house to watch football. You're in a hurry because you don't want to miss kickoff, and you have to stop at the nearest cash machine first, because you promised to bring the beer. But instead of cash, the ATM commandeers your card, rudely informing you that it has expired.

Furious, but knowing you won't get much help on a holiday, you head to the nearest 7-11 intending to pay for your refreshments with a credit card. Pulling up to the store, you think a lot of people have the same idea, because there's a long line at the checkout counter. But the problem is not a run on beer; instead, you find out, the cash register is not working. The word, as it reaches you at the end of the line, is that the cash register is computer-based and requires a valid date to start up. And for some reason, it won't. "Some reason" is the Year 2000 problem, Y2K for short.

The preceding hypothetical—but probable—scenario is just the tip of the iceberg, and if collective public denial continues, it is an iceberg that will sink titanic computer systems worldwide. Like the unheeded warnings of disaster on the ocean liner *Titanic*, the alert to the Year 2000 problem has been sounded—on television, in newspapers, magazines, and newsletters, and via the Internet. Often, however, it has been defined simply as the inability of computers to calculate properly with 00—two zeros—signifying the new century. Further, media coverage frequently couches the issue in computer jargon, making it seem irrelevant to anyone other than programmers and information systems managers. The truth is, the Year 2000 problem will affect each of us, personally and professionally.

What is the Year 2000 problem? It is not one, but a series of problems, some involving computer software, some involving computer hardware, some involving data, and *all* involving large amounts of money to fix. The nature of these problems is easily explained. Until 1989, all the standards followed to create computer programs stated that only two digits—the last two—would be used to identify the year, and to date this has been an efficient abbreviation. But at the dawn of the millennium—when 2000 will be recorded as 00—most computers will regard 2000 as 1900. Thus, computers will treat a driver's license, credit card, passport, or drug prescription that is due to expire in the year 2000 as already having done so.

Happy Birthday

To understand the disruptions this will cause, it is essential to remember that computers were not designed to do arithmetic but to perform operations involving logic. For example, to determine that a person born in 1945 was older than a person born in 1955, a computer would calculate ages and then compare them. In 1995, the calculations were simple: $95 - 45 = 50$, $95 - 55 = 40$; 50 compared to 40 is greater. But in the year 2000, these calculations stop working correctly: $00 - 45 = 45$, $00 - 55 = 55$; the computer identifies the older person as being younger. But keep in mind that last equation should include minus signs, thus: $00 - 45 = -45$, and $00 - 55 = -55$; the calculations *should* still work. And that would be true if all those early programs had been designed to maintain plus and minus signs when doing calculations on dates. But they weren't. Why not? Simply put, these programs weren't intended to run beyond the twentieth century.

Let's take a look at a couple of birthday surprises already caused by the upcoming new year. Brian Hayes, in his article "Waiting for 01-01-00" in *American Scientist* (January/February 1995), gives these two examples of potentially typical, albeit humorous, repercussions of the Year 2000 problem.

> In 1992 Mary Bandar of Winona, Minnesota, was invited to join kindergarten classes when her name turned up among others identified in a database search for people born in '88; at the time Bandar was 104 years old.
>
> C. G. Blodgett's auto-insurance premium tripled when he was reclassified after his 101st birthday as a high-risk youthful driver.

Don't, however, be lulled into thinking that these anecdotes are interesting only as sound bites during the feel-good portion of a nightly newscast. They are symptomatic of potential worldwide disruptions in business, transportation, finance, and much more. Let's get a little more serious.

Say you make a deposit to your personal or business bank account at the end of 1999, then write a check or make a transfer in 2000. If the bank's computer regards 00 in the date field as 1900 (as most do), it will treat the withdrawal as if it were made *before* the deposit, and your personal and/or business accounts will be overdrawn. Now are you beginning to see the problem?

Another dilemma is that back in the good ol' days, when people thought 2000 was a long time away, programmers felt safe using the

digit pairs 00 and 99 to indicate either "keep forever" or "delete now."
Thus, 99 is commonly used to terminate processing. One organization realized nearly six months into 1994 that its computer was dis-
carding files that were supposed to be stored for the next five years
because it was programmed to purge data with 99 in the year field.

Storage space intended for dates has long been used and abused.
One retailer, while investigating the possibility of a computer crime,
discovered that the year values 94, 95, 96, and 97 were being used to
indicate that discounts of various amounts were to be applied. And
although some foresighted companies had specified that date fields
were to include space for the century, programmers had done
nothing to verify that it was done. Worse, in some instances they
found that the space had been used to store other data.

Leap of Math

Now consider the following: Shortly after February 29, 1988, a
supermarket was fined $1,000 for having meat around one day too
long. The problem was traced to a computer that didn't adjust for the
leap year. What does this have to do with the Year 2000? Read on.

To determine what to do, computer programs refer to internal
calendars, most of which were designed to run only through the
twentieth century. And while 1900 was not a leap year, 2000 is. If
you're as confused as most programmers about how to determine
this, here are the three rules for determining a leap year: Rule 1 says
that if the year is evenly divisible by 4, it is a leap year. Since 2000 is
divisible evenly by 4, it must be a leap year. Not so fast. Rule 2 says it
isn't a leap year if the year is also divisible by 100. And 2000 is divisible by 100 as well as 4. So it isn't a leap year, right? Wrong again.
There's rule 3: When the year is also divisible by 400, it is a leap year
and does have a February 29, which includes 2000 (technically, it's a
leap-century day). If, when 2000 arrives, your computer treats it as

1900, it won't account for February 29, because there wasn't one that year. Needless to say, there are many computer calendars out there in which every month will be off one day following New Year 2000. Consider the implications of that on computers that are dependent on date data to manipulate security systems, traffic signals, train and airplane arrival and departure information, surgery schedules at hospitals.

Up from Denial

Make no mistake about it, the Year 2000 problem is starting to generate considerable attention. Nevertheless, Ed Yourdon, editor of *Application Development Strategies* and a widely renowned information systems specialist, conducted an informal survey that convinced him that this attention has not translated into appropriate levels of concern. His impressions were supported in a May 23, 1996, article in *Washington Technology,* which indicated that two-thirds of the "infotech" executives surveyed believed the Year 2000 problem was not a high priority, three-fourths of program officials believed it wasn't a high priority, and one-half of information technology executives planned to wait until 1998 to take action. Finally, a survey in the February 1996 issue of *Information Week* indicated that 50 percent of the U.S. data processing organizations will not have their software converted by December 31, 1999.

And of those corporations that are actively engaged in solving this problem, most are not speaking out about their efforts. Neil Cooper, a stock analyst with Cruttenden Roth who is working on the Year 2000 problem, offered the following reasons for this conspiracy of silence:

- Directors and management are fearful of shareholder suits claiming negligence—many employee warnings have gone unheeded for years.

- Acknowledgment of a serious Year 2000 problem within a business unit or across an enterprise may cause clients to flee and competitors to flock.
- The legal ramifications remain unclear for consulting services companies that have provided hardware and software solutions that did not include Year 2000 fixes in the recent past. Generally, both (potential) plaintiffs and defendants will not comment if litigation is being considered.
- Some companies are awaiting the leadership of regulatory agencies and/or financial accounting standards bodies within the federal government for this unique one-time event.

Fortunately, not all organizations are waiting for the ball to drop in Times Square to tackle this issue. A number of companies have completed the initial project-estimating phase, although few have embarked on the fixing stage. Many are still suffering from what car buyers refer to as "sticker shock." Others are trying to determine which computer applications must be saved, which will cost less to replace than fix, and which can be fixed as they break down. Still other companies are so dependent upon computer hardware and software purchased from other companies that they must wait until the vendors address their own internally developed programs.

At Massachusetts Mutual Life Insurance Co., Ron Cote, a Year 2000 project leader, calls his effort a "survival project." "If we don't do this," he says, "it's shut the lights off and go home." So far, the workarounds developed by their information systems people have proved unsatisfactory, and they have 45 million lines of code to change and then to test. Mass Mutual wants to complete its project by the end of 1998, which will provide a one-year cushion. The company has been aware of this problem for more than 10 years.

It is important to realize that many industries have become totally dependent on computers to function. Insurance companies, banks, securities brokers, and many more have become data processing firms. They get data, send data, and use data to function. Without their computers, they simply would not be able to conduct business. And computers that are not programmed to accept values of 00 in the year field will not run. Don't forget, computer applications are highly integrated. Data from one application often is required for the next to run successfully. If the first one doesn't run because it confronts a value containing 99 or 00, any program dependent on it won't run, either; call it the domino effect.

Complicating the situation is that many programs run in strings, making it difficult to determine which program failed. Finding the problem in the first might only get you to the next in the string, which might subsequently fail. And each failure may take hours to correct. The system failures ultimately overwhelm the people who can correct them. If these problems occur in systems taking orders, paying claims, or issuing paychecks, the companies dependent on them will quickly lose credibility and be in violation of regulations.

Consider the city of Phoenix, which found out about the Year 2000 the hard way. On January 2, 1995, a simple application that calculated five-year payments crashed. When the program tried to subtract 95 from 00, it couldn't handle it. Jack Thomas, the city's information systems deputy director, considers the crash a blessing in disguise, for if the application hadn't failed, the city could have begun calculating inaccurate payment schedules with potentially disastrous results.

An analysis by Viasoft, a tools contractor that began tackling the problem in Phoenix in 1994, found that more than 90 percent of the city's programs use date routines that cause problems. He estimated it would cost that municipality $63 million to fix its Year 2000 problem throughout 14 major applications that support several major city departments.

Financial services companies that know they will be impacted by the Year 2000 problem include Abbey National, Lloyd's of London, Barclays, and NatWest—and that's just in Great Britain. This, naturally, comes at the same time that work must progress for conversion to a single European currency unit—ECU. Other countries in the community, of course, will be facing the same dilemma.

Other institutions and companies that have invested in fixing their Year 2000 problem include many banks: Bank of Boston, Canadian Imperial Bank of Commerce, Fleet Bank, Nations Bank, and Sun Bank among them. Manufacturers such as Philip Morris, Shell Services, and Texaco (to name just a few) are also engaged in correcting the problem. Some firms, such as Kaiser Permanente and Union Pacific (both of which have participated in important conferences and roundtables on the Year 2000 in order to share what they have learned), have already begun, or are close to completing, conversion of their computers to cope with the Year 2000 problem.

- In 1991, the northern California division of Kaiser Permanente started setting up a team of about 20 outside contractors and 10 internal staff to begin working through their computer applications. They expanded date fields to allow for century values, then added the century values to all their current data; they also backtracked into historical data to add the century values. They removed all queries to the hardware manufacturer's date routines and installed their own. Finally, they created a standard set of date-processing routines and replaced all others with them.

- In 1995, Union Pacific hired a consulting firm to assess the approximate cost of fixing its computer systems to handle the new century. In 1996, it commenced its project. In some cases, the update team expanded the date fields to support century values and changed the data. In others, they inserted logical date interpretation processes so as not to change the data.

- The Bank of Boston set up a special staff to perform date-field expansions. The application support teams send programs to the staff, who expand the fields and replace date routines with standard routines. Any logical processes that must be changed are identified; the altered programs are returned, along with programs to handle data changes to the application support teams who must change the programs to fix the logic problems and test them.

As always, when someone loses, someone wins. It is easy to imagine that some firms are already building war chests, to acquire companies that fail to survive the countdown to double-zero. In fact, more than one company insider has indicated that it is a strategy under discussion. Some companies are already benefiting from their lead in fixing the problem. Kaiser Permanente won a corporate contract for group health coverage when its nearest competitor confessed that it was doing nothing to prepare for the year 2000.

Are you starting to wonder how you and your company or organization will be affected? So far, there are no "silver bullet" solutions to the Year 2000 problem, although certainly many hope for such an easy way out, exemplified in this statement in the August 3, 1996, issue of *The Economist:* "This is doubtless a technical feat that Microsoft or some other firm will shortly master." Microsoft was having enough trouble dealing with the most recent "fall back" to daylight savings. As reported in *PC Week* on November 4, 1996, in Spencer Katt's "Rumor Central," at 2:00 A.M. on the morning of daylight savings' Sunday, those who turned their computer clocks back (as prompted on-screen) discovered that one hour later, it was 1:00 A.M. again. Fortunately, few people were up working at that hour. The point is, it would be foolhardy to wait for anyone to deliver the quick fix to the Year 2000 problem.

But it can be solved—today. Like a genetic disorder, the solution lies in finding each mistake in the code—in this case, program code—and fixing it. The bad news is, the code is often difficult to find and thus to correct. The good news is, enterprises that are well into the millennium update are already reaping significant benefits.

Some have won new contracts simply because they can demonstrate preparations are in process. In some situations, budgets that have been restricted over the last few years are being relaxed, allowing organizations to upgrade systems software and hardware. Fixing the Year 2000 problem will enable growth of new functions and potentially decrease support costs.

Our goal in this book is twofold: (1) to convince you that a problem does exist that will affect you and your business and (2) to give you the insight into how to start doing something about it.

Chapter One

Ground Double-Zero

S o much anthropomorphic terminology has found its way into the computer technology lexicon that we forget computers are machines: they can't really "think" or "see," and they don't really "know" anything. When *we* see the date 01/01/00, we *know* it refers to January 1, 2000; when the computer "sees" 01/01/00, it "knows" it is January 1, 1900; or it might "know" to delete the information accompanying the double-zero number string. The upcoming dawn of the millennium is going to require that we stop trusting our computer systems to know anything other than what we have programmed them to know. It is time to take responsibility for not being far-sighted enough to plan for their future use beyond the year 1999.

Programming began on punch cards known as Hollerith cards, named for the man who invented them in the late 1800s in order to get the U.S. Census done on time. Each Hollerith card had only 80 columns, and all information for each record had to fit into those 80 columns. How could early programmers have guessed that one of the shortcuts they developed to accommodate that 80-column restriction would one day result in a data nightmare? To save space for more important information, early on, the year designation was reduced to two digits, the assumption—then rightfully—being that everyone knew the century prefix was 19.

Over the last 50 years, we have gone through countless upgrades of computer technology. At some point, you or your enterprise wanted or needed some feature that required a new computer. The decision was made, the budget was secured, and you bought the new model. The old one was sent to some computer equivalent of an elephant burial ground. You remember what came next: conversion, the process during which you tried to get old programs to run on new equipment. Code was written on the fly, often without documentation, to keep the system up and running.

Through all these years and all these conversions and upgrades, we have been stuffing an ever increasing amount of data into computers. We have tons of it stored on disks and tapes, in huge vaults, and in closets and caves. We also have duplicate data, because most key files are duplicated daily. There are even copies of copies. And for the most part, we have stored this data in large files in date sequence according to when it was collected. Many of the structural programs—the ones that handle physical resources such as tape and disk management, scheduling and communications—can't manage a four-digit year at all. Business applications depend on these structural systems. If they can't figure out how old you are, how long an invoice has gone unpaid, which transaction should be processed first, or how much interest the bank owes, the companies that depend on them are in big trouble.

Out of the Closet

These "closets" full of old data complicate the challenge of making the programs and computers in daily use Year 2000–compliant. Few companies have maintained conscientious code documentation; fewer still can boast that the programmer who wrote it is still on staff. Without documentation, without the programmer(s), the solution is easy to describe, but mind-boggling to implement: Examine and correct each and every line of code and then fix the digit-deficient data residing in all data files, or write new systems able to handle the problem. A single program could have from 10 (a 4GL program) to 100,000 lines of code, and 1 in 20 lines of code have something to do with defining or processing date data. In terms of functions performed, this means that nearly 5 percent of all data processing operations are impacted by dates. If you look at a medium-size organization with 4 million lines of code, it will have to visually scan, one by one, every line to find 200,000 instances of date usage. It will then have to make approximately 20,000 changes, requiring not less than 13 hours (based on our prior experience in making a similar enterprisewide update) to design test data, create a program to build the test data, and run the tests for each group of about 10 changes. This means that it will require 26,000 hours (roughly 18 person-years of uninterrupted attention—no coffee breaks, training, waiting for equipment, or downtime) to make and test all changes. Then you have to factor in the misses: Every time a change is missed, it will take four to six hours to find and "patch" the code. And don't forget, the changes must be scheduled in the proper sequence. At any one point in time, it may be necessary to have 60 people making changes so that all interrelated programs are altered simultaneously. Conversely, at another time, only one person may be able to make a change so that 60 others can start working together.

The cost of accommodating all that old data is staggering. According to the combined research of Ken Orr in Topeka, Kansas, and Larry Martin, president of Data Dimensions Inc., in Bellevue, Washington, an early estimate for Fortune 50 organizations puts the figure between $50 million and $100 million each to convert all existing and developing systems to accept the change from the 1999 to 2000. All that old data either must be changed or someone must go into every program and put in some code that essentially says, "If the year is greater than 49 and less than 99, pretend that there is a 19 in front of it." Easier said than done. Some dates are not so easy to expand, which brings us to the issue of embedded dates and date stamping.

Getting Embed with Dates

Embedded systems are everywhere. We have put computers of a wide range of capabilities into more and more of the equipment we use daily. A lot of people are wearing fancy watches that do all kinds of nifty things with calendars. Some of those will stop working when the date rolls over on December 31, 1999. Those in your VCR may cause minimal problems, as there's nothing to record between midnight and 8 A.M. on January 1 anyway. If you plan to set your recorder to catch a game, though, you should check it to see if it works (assuming you know how to program your VCR in the first place).

Embedded business systems control lights, elevators, security systems, time clocks, and heating and cooling systems. They are in the scales in receiving, in conveyors on the shop floor, and in emissions-monitoring and waste-removal systems. They control cutters, moulders, and pressers. They turn lights on and off in your parking garages and lots. They are in the monitoring equipment in hospital operating rooms. In short, embedded systems control the conditions in which you work; sometimes they even determine *whether* you work.

The problem with embedded systems is that they run in the background, and currently most are running in obsolete equipment. This means that you can rarely just reprogram them; you have to replace processors, circuit boards, and sometimes the whole unit—a major expense, needless to say. Banks, for example, have been finding that not only do some of their ATMs have to be replaced, but also the kiosks in which they are mounted, because the new units are smaller than the older, bulkier ones.

Embedded systems are one problem; embedded dates are another. An embedded date is one that is used as a component of a longer character string to uniquely identify a particular item or event. Embedded dates are commonly found in invoice numbers, such as 94090013, where 9409 is the year and month of issue. They also appear as parts of policy numbers, license numbers, merchandise sales tags, storage bin tags, transaction numbers, and date stamps.

These dates are built into the data that you retain and use daily. The worst of these appear in the key fields you use to determine where and in what order you store data. Others appear in date stamps you use to track data and processing actions. Embedded dates typically appear in four formats:

Type	Format	Common Usage
Prefix	YYMMXXXX	Invoice #
Suffix	XXXXYYMM	Policy #
Encapsulated	XXYYMMXX	License #
Date/time stamp	XXX-YYMMDD-HHMMSS.SS or YYMMDD-HHMMSS.SS-XXX	Transaction Identification

When dates appear at the beginning or end of the field, they are often used for "intelligence"—to provide the observer with status information. When a field contains an embedded date, the following questions must be answered:

1. Is it used to determine item aging or age?
2. Is it used to sort the item into sequence?
3. Is there a calculation being made?

For example, one apparel retailer that uses dates as a prefix to its stock item numbers spent several million dollars on encoding and scanning equipment that could read the garment number. But because the scanners had a limitation on the length of the scan, the date field could not be lengthened; the other characters and digits were equally significant and could not be dropped or truncated. So if the century field could not be added, all this retailer's inventory dated 99 or earlier could not be tracked correctly, meaning they wouldn't be aged for distribution, disposition, or markdown. Unsurprisingly, this retailer prefers to remain nameless.

DATE STAMPING

Date stamping is another intelligent use of embedded dates in records. Date stamps are automatically placed on the record by the system for such things as transaction tracing and backup recovery. However, date stamps often create problems as the formats change; for example, old data is not recognized by the new recovery routines. If changes are not made, the transactions or records may be processed out of sequence. The result could be as described by Brian Hayes in *American Scientist* (January/February 1995):

> At the local dairy, the oldest milk on hand is supposed to be shipped first, but in the early weeks of the new millennium milk from year 00 is given precedence. Indeed, any milk remaining from December 1999 will not be scheduled for shipment until the end of 2099. Meanwhile, at the bakery across town a computer calculates the bread dated 01-01-00 must be a century old, and sends it to the landfill.

> Extend these examples to blood donations, medicine, prescriptions, medical records . . . and you have genuine disasters in the making once 00 makes its way into the data stream.

Certainly code can be fixed for applications created in standard languages, which are well understood by a sizable number of programmers. However, when some "unique" language such as JOVIAL or APL is involved, costs increase dramatically because of competition for rare resources. Which brings us to one of the key issues in the Year 2000 problem.

No Comprendo COBOL

By some estimates, the number of computer languages in use totals more than 300, including various coding dialects. A few major languages, such as COBOL, BASIC, FORTRAN, and C, probably account for 80 percent of the programs running today, but each has several dialects and versions. Fortunately, most of these are relatively easy to understand, and if a programmer knows one dialect, he or she can learn the others.

Other languages, however, are more obscure, either because so few programmers ever learned the language, or the language enabled the programmer to write in a way that kept the code inaccessible and thereby tamperproof. Thus, in one such program you might see the letter A used to signify a storage location for a person's name and B used to identify date of birth. In the next program, you might find the same letters used to identify something totally different. (One programmer we knew actually bragged that his efficiency was due to the reduction in keystrokes it required for him to write programs. Imagine a whole system in which the programmer kept the whole system's data mapping in his head.)

Other update complications are based on original attempts to save space, while still others relate to the attempt to reduce the costs of data storage and communications. Compression of numeric data and zero suppression on computer terminals are examples.

A few attempts to save costs have resulted in imaginative data storage strategies. People have confronted situations where the dates *look* encrypted: A year may be assigned the value of A, the next year B, and so on. These date formats are referred to as *interpreted*. The format of the field may appear as YDDD, where Y has an alphanumeric, or even symbolic, value. In other formats of YMDD, both year and month appear with values of 0 to 9 or A through Z. This is, by some measures, very efficient. The single digit gives the system a date range of up to 36 years. Surely every program should have been replaced by then?

Where different versions of the same language exist, the issue is one of effort. Old versions of compilers are not maintained. For example, IBM mainframe COBOL has been changed only in the two most recent releases to accommodate century information. This means that all older releases are not able to read the new dates using the IBM-supplied routines. Upgrading those older releases means that the companies have to go through many thousands of additional hours of work (which is why they weren't changed in the first place).

Dates appearing at the beginning of the identifier create another difficulty. Some application software automatically suppresses leading zeros in numeric field, causing miscalculations because 00 may be treated as null data and thus be rejected or result in a calculation or zero-divide error.

Then there's the problem of language obsolescence. Many languages are literally dead. They continue to work, but nobody knows how to change them—and even if you could find someone to change them, there may be no compiler or interpreter still available to turn them into functional code that the computer can understand. Example: IBM created a product called ADF in Europe in the early 1980s. Several million lines of code were written in the language. In 1989, IBM abandoned ADF. Consequently "Big Blue" won't (can't) fix it to handle four-digit year designations, and running the programs requires having an active interpreter on the computer at the same time. The interpreter doesn't handle century dates. What does a company still using ADF do? Its choices: Completely rewrite the code (assuming someone knows what it does); figure a way to fool the interpreter and insert that logic everywhere it is required (assuming you can find enough programmers and train them); find a way to convert the code to COBOL (one does exist, we're told) and then convert it (assuming you can afford the time to find the vendor, learn how to use the tool, convert the programs, and make the changes before the system collapses). There are approximately 200 other obsolete and/or unsupported languages.

In addition, in old programs you have the challenge of locating the source code. And assuming you locate the source code, can you be sure it is the same version that created the programs you are currently running on the computer? Probably not. You could be forced to re-create programs whose functions are no longer understood by anyone in your organization.

Counting the Costs

Computers have worked astoundingly well for us in the past. They will do so again in the future. But between now and then we will all be in for a wild, rocky, and expensive ride.

It may seem inconceivable that a couple of zeros in a date could multiply so dramatically into some very large repair bills, but that is what will happen as you prepare to fix the Year 2000 problem. To ease you into this awareness, let's discuss "controllable" costs, which fall into two subcategories: (1) internally developed computer systems and (2) business practices and operations.

APPLICATION SOFTWARE

Most organizations have a large number of internally developed programs. For instance, at a conference on the Year 2000 problem in April

1996, Union Pacific revealed it had nearly 9,000 programs in just one category. These 8,790 programs had 16.2 *million* lines of code.

The first problem, as we've already touched on, is that in many cases no one in any given organization knows where these programs are located. It is not unusual for programmers' original code to be stored in public and private libraries or in archive files that are not even on the computer. Programmers actually keep tapes in their desk drawers. Thus, it is also not unusual for a programming department to require three months or longer to find the code they own. If and when they do find it, often they are not sure what it is they have found.

You will learn, if you don't already know it, that the program versions running on your computer are not always the same ones that match the code you found. Consequently, you will have to hire or delegate someone (perhaps several people) to find these missing program versions and match up the programs running with the programmer-created code. To a noncomputer person, all this talk of code, source, and compilers may be confusing, so please allow a minor digression.

Programs are written in a language relatively friendly to humans. It can be expressed in letters, numbers, words. Values may require special forms, wherein the form translates into directions. Which gets us to the point: The language in which a program is written is not actionable by a computer. This requires that the code (which is why it is called *source code*) be assembled, compiled, or interpreted into machine language (*machine code*). This is put into production libraries. The source code used to create the machine code is *supposed* to be filed away so that the machine code can be replaced if it gets accidentally destroyed or corrupted. In an ideal situation, the source and machine code are kept at the same level. Needless to say, however, the ideal situation is rare indeed. The older the machine code, the more likely that its source code will become corrupted (changes made but not put into production, source code lost and an old version brought up from archives, or the source code is simply misplaced and nobody realizes it). Unless you can recompile (assemble or interpret) the code and fully test it, it is unlikely that you can spot any obvious problems until it is run in production. And because changes are incremental, the differences can be very subtle.

If there are inconsistencies between what is being run today and the versions that were saved in 1992, for example, your designated troubleshooter is going to have to spend time re-creating the changes that have taken place between the versions. In addition, lost programs and code will have to be re-created or restored—if possible. It is important to start thinking early about buying software packages to replace lost code—another expense.

THE COST OF THE UPDATE

The first order of business in estimating your code update/reconstruction cost is to determine how many lines of code you must account for. If you are able to locate all your code, you will be relieved to know that it is possible to obtain line counts using the computer. Source code is usually stored in libraries on the computer. Production versions of the machine language are in *runtime* or *object libraries*. The names of these programs can be matched to the names on the members of the source libraries. This allows you to determine which source code modules are in use. Other modules are not shown in the object libraries because they are "linked" or included during compilation, assembly, or interpretation. To find which of these are in use, it is possible to match the source library names found to the *link libraries*. A similar operation is used to find modules brought together by interpreters, but the method varies by product.

While you will see forecasts of from $.60 to $1.70 per line of code, this is an aggregate estimate for the entire code portfolio, including vendor-supplied code and control language code. Industry estimates for the cost of updating individual programs and applications (a group of programs with a single business purpose) of course vary significantly—from absolutely nothing to as much as $4.50 per line of code. Individual programs may not require any changes since they do not involve date processes. Many manufacturing companies use an artificial date that cycles every 20 or 30 years. These systems do not require many changes. Remember, we are talking about the wide variability in the cost of changing individual programs and applications—not the entire portfolio. The Department of Defense, for example, estimates that some of its code will cost up to $8.05 per line. The industrywide average is probably somewhere around $1.50 per line. Naturally, there is economy in scale of operation, so smaller enterprises will probably have to pay as little as $.50 or as much as $2.50 per line. Complexity is a critical factor: Those applications that interact with a lot of other applications or that were written in arcane languages are more difficult to change (the Department of Defense estimate reflects costs for JOVIAL, hardly a popular computer language). If you want a rule of thumb to determine where you stand in these ranges, we suggest that you consider the following five attributes in the order presented:

1. Available staff knowledge of the application
2. Amount of planning prior to update
3. Capability of project management and level of enterprise awareness
4. Tools and methods that can be employed
5. Complexity of the applications

To ascertain an accurate estimate, it's best to hire an experienced organization to do it for you. It may be far more objective than your staff in its assessment of the factors mentioned. Companies offering help in estimating the Year 2000 problem include the following:

CAPGemini
CGI Group

Computer Horizons

Coopers & Lybrand Technologies

Data Dimensions, Inc.

Ernst & Young LLP

IBM

KPMG Peat Marwick LLP

SPR, Inc.

Viasoft, Inc.

The computer platforms and languages they support vary widely. Some limit their services to IBM MVS COBOL. Tools are available for purchase that can be run by the customer to spot date code, but these do not include estimating capability. A search of tools can often be a frustrating process. You may want to find a silver bullet, but none exists, and the number of tools you may eventually need to implement is surprising. We will expand on this topic in Chapters 8 and 9.

Because many enterprises have several hundred million lines of code, their cost to fix this problem will run into millions of dollars— all to be spent in the next couple of years. If, for instance, your programming department staff consists of 20 people, they are probably supporting about 4 to 6 million lines of code. Using an increasing average cost of $100,000 per person-year, those 4 to 6 million lines of code will take about 40 to 60 person-years and $2 to $3 million in expenses to fix. In other words, the Year 2000 problem is your first, second, third, fourth, and fifth priority.

Let's suppose your company has 100 million lines of code on your computer system (this is not an uncommon amount). The more code you have, the more money per line you're probably going to spend, because all of it no doubt interacts with everything else. Thus, when somebody changes one line, it will impact something else, and more changes will have to be made to make it work (and don't forget, you still have to keep your customers happy while this repair work is going on).

COUNTING OTHER COSTS

Don't be misled by the preceding discussion into thinking, as so many have, that the Year 2000 problem is only a budget issue and that you will deal with it when you can finesse the dollars to do so. It is not just a budget issue; it is a scheduling problem, a skill problem, a resource problem, a testing problem, a management problem, and, most important, a time problem. Simply put, we're running out of time. According to Data Dimensions, the code must all be fixed by September 30, 1998, in order to allow enough time to test and run the code prior to 2000. And Data Dimensions should know. In 1991, it began making Year 2000 changes, and within a year, that became the firm's single business focus. It has worked with an ever growing number of major firms in making changes and has assisted more than 200 firms in planning for making the changes over the last four years. It has estimated the impact of the date change on over 70 computer languages, scanning over 3 billion lines of code and putting back into production more than 20 million lines of code that is date-compliant, using both four-digit-year and two-digit-year solutions. Its planning, preparation, and update processes are used in over 35 countries from Israel and Saudi Arabia to Australia, South Africa, and Finland. For more on this firm, access http://www.data-dimensions.com.

Again, these are all controllable costs. You decide what and when you are going to change. You decide if you are not going to change a system but replace it. You have choices to make, but the decisions are yours.

The uncontrollable business practices costs will depend on the nature of your enterprise. For example:

- Banks that lend money to businesses will want to know what those businesses are doing to prepare for the year 2000. Loan officers will need to know what information to look for.

- Manufacturers of devices that incorporate computers in their products will have to determine how to help their customers reprogram those units that are obsolete.

- Businesses dependent on suppliers will have to ascertain those suppliers' readiness. Are they business partners? Will it be part of your responsibility to help them make the transitions necessary to 2000?

- If you buy computer hardware and software, do you want to stop purchases of any products that are not 2000-ready? Perhaps you should put into place a process that forces vendors to prove their products will not have date-handling problems.

- Processes that are computer controlled should be tested for date-sensitivity.

- Large enterprises may want to create a single coordination point—assign a project manager—to ensure that all changes are planned and scheduled to achieve efficiency and avoid system breakdowns between branches.

- Vendors of perishable products (prescription drugs, etc.) dated 00 will have to design workarounds to ensure safety—and to prevent potential lawsuits.

- Service providers will need to determine the extent of their liability if their systems fail.

Everything, obviously, depends on *when* you begin.

TICK, TICK

The longer you wait, the greater the risk to your enterprise and the greater the cost to alleviate that risk. Programmer repair costs mount daily with the ticking of the millennial clock. The competition for qualified people in this area is growing fierce. Many consulting firms engaged in the Year 2000 update are already raiding each other for experienced technicians and managers. This trend will continue to drive up costs.

Let's review a typical case of an organization with 15 million lines of mainframe code and 2 million lines of code on other platforms. We'll assume that the planning started on January 2, 1997, and the final system is to be migrated by December 31, 1998. Here's a breakdown of the process:

Time	Phase	Resources
1997 Jan.–Mar.	Sizing	12 staff months
1997 Jan.–June	Planning	12 staff months
1997 Apr.–July	Pilots	50 staff months
July 1997–Dec. 1998	Update	1,800 staff months

Beginning in 1997, the overlapping of phase activities becomes necessary. It is important to be finished by the end of 1998 to allow the changes you've made to be run in production through daily, weekly, monthly, quarterly, and year-end cycles. The crucial period of this plan is the update. During those 18 months, the enterprise will have to commit 100 people to the task.

If you are not into the update process by July 1997, the time line is reduced significantly, and the resource requirement changes dramatically. A delay of three months requires the addition of 20 people. For every process that is delayed, the impact may be the loss of several precious months. If you cannot find or devote those resources, the price may be the collapse of many applications. Bottom line: If you don't meet the deadline, the deadline will meet you. Your enterprise is already in jeopardy.

Costs You Can't Control

Now it's time to tackle costs outside your immediate domain; those outside factors can bring down your enterprise, even if you do have all your internal applications upgraded and 2000-ready.

VENDORS

The first order of business is to alert your vendors to your needs. Begin by getting answers to the following questions immediately:

- Have my vendors recognized the millennium date problem?
- Will my vendors fix their problems before my business processes require century dates?
- Can my vendors afford to fix their products, or will they abandon them?
- What approaches will my vendors take, and will they be consistent with my standards or force me to customize my processes?
- What will be the cost, resource requirement, and time available when I get their solutions?
- Are my vendors dependent on other suppliers that may not perform or may not perform in time?
- How much are my vendors' solutions going to cost me, and when will we have to pay for it?

Vendors requiring management include suppliers of computers and computer-based devices that contain software, operating systems, applications software, data management, utilities, and tools, as well as suppliers of information on electronic media—data importers.

We recommend the following steps to establish control of the vendors (courtesy of Data Dimensions as reported in the Millennium Journal, Volume II.I).

1. Centralize vendor management responsibility.
2. Set vendor policies for new acquisitions.
3. Determine whether changes are required for each purchased product.
4. Establish the event horizons for each product.
5. Identify the current vendor for each product.
6. Build a vendor database.
7. Determine contractual responsibility.
8. Contact the vendor for plans.
9. Plan implementation steps.
10. Communicate the vendor's and your own implementation plans to others who need to know.

One proactive manager of a testing laboratory in a client/server environment found that he had 14 vendors of hardware and software products. Once he defined his needs for each vendor, it took him about two and a half years to achieve compliance. Specifically, it required individual meetings with each vendor to explain the problem. Then each vendor was asked to test its products and schedule the necessary change. In some cases, this required reprogramming application software; in others, it also meant changing the data output. The biggest problem was in scheduling which changes would be implemented. Certain vendors finished before others, while in other cases the changes didn't work and the vendors had to repair them.

Unfortunately, if you are a large corporation you might have 10,000 vendors for which to define requirements and track for compliance. But regardless of the size of your enterprise, there are four categories of suppliers that you must be concerned about:

- Application software
- Computer hardware and system software
- Embedded systems
- Service providers

Application Software

Application software packages and programs that you bought from vendors present several potential problems.

- The nature of the fast-paced, ever changing computer industry has resulted in companies going in and out of business before you have a chance to add their cards to your Rolodex. Others will bite the dust as a result of the Year 2000 problem. Thus you may find that the vendor from whom you bought your software is no longer in business and available to help with your transition.

- If you stopped paying for maintenance for a number of the products you are still running, you may have to reinstate the contract to obtain the upgrades. And be aware that some vendors will charge several years' maintenance fees. You may also have difficulty integrating new features or functions that were added. And even if you kept your maintenance contract current, you may find that your vendor does not have the knowledge or staff to fix your code.

- Expect a number of vendors to simply declare your products as "unsupported" and stop charging maintenance fees. Of course, this leaves you holding nothing. If you are lucky, the vendor may be able to provide the source code so your staff can fix it.

- If your vendors tell you they plan to fix the code, the first question to ask is, "When?" The second question is, "Will it coincide with my needs?" That second question will most likely have two answers, one determined by how much internally developed code must be changed because of the vendor's revisions. The second answer depends on how you're using dates within the system. You may need the changes earlier than the vendor can provide them.

Computer Hardware and Systems Software

Hardware vendors provide the systems software that the computer uses to run, and this software is full of dates. You will be relieved to know that most systems software is either already compliant or in the process of being made so, although some of these fixes are not scheduled to be implemented until 1999.

Unfortunately, as with some application software vendors, some equipment vendors, too, may declare their software as "unsupported," meaning that the vendor will not make the changes. Usually this is the case when a vendor does not have enough customers to justify the expense.

In many cases, the hardware issue is complicated because companies have chosen to stay with an older system to avoid the cost of upgrading, and therefore any Year 2000 changes will be to a version that they are unequipped to install. According to the Portland *Oregonian,* in early August 1996, an untested computer system went into service during the Department of Motor Vehicles' busiest season. The manager resigned amid an uproar following her estimate that it would cost $75 million for the new computer system (estimates are now running closer to $123 million), which was originally estimated at $48 million. Ironically, one of the reasons testing may have been put on the back burner by the agency was because of workforce reductions that were made in anticipation of labor savings from the new computer system.

Embedded Systems

As we've already mentioned, embedded systems are everywhere, and most are running in obsolete equipment. You won't be able to reprogram them; you'll have to replace them. Be prepared for unexpected failures in systems you thought were free of this problem.

Service Providers

Obviously, you need supplies to keep your business going. Retail stores, for example, are concerned about whether the bank credit approval systems will be working, whether their lights will go on, and whether the cash registers will work. Lack of supplies will stop them cold. McDonald's, for one, is so concerned that it created a project and hired outside help to assist its suppliers and franchise operators to get their systems ready. It recognized that its franchisees and suppliers were essential to maintaining its income stream. McDonald's began by investigating the food preparation and order-taking equipment used by the outlets. It then put its franchisees and store operators on notice about what the options were and began to contact all its suppliers to determine to what extent each was dependent on computing. Currently, McDonald's is proceeding to make recommendations as to what each should do and is setting up a process to track progress.

The best advice is to contact your service providers now to determine which ones you can count on. And get verification—proof. Don't take anyone's word that they are 2000-ready.

Chapter Two

Behind Every Great Machine

By now, the enormity of the Y2K problem should be obvious to you. Some of you may have your calculators out, trying to do the math for your enterprise—figuring how many programs and how much data you have on what kind of machines and how much it will cost to fix or replace it all. At this point, however, stop adding up the numbers and start evaluating this problem first as one of management, because although Y2K is obviously a costly technical problem, until you get the people together who can take you into 2000 with champagne in hand, you're nowhere. In this chapter, we're going to talk management first—finding, forming, and coordinating a Year 2000 management team. Then we'll talk about all those 2000-resistant machines.

Creating management awareness of the Year 2000 problem means launching people into a proactive stance, thus empowering them. The following are several areas you will need to consider before you set up your team:

- *Staff to locate "lost" processes and products.* We have been purchasing equipment for years that contains computers as integrated components. All of these now have to be identified and studied to determine if they will require repair, reprogramming, or replacement. Some companies producing these components have changed name, moved, and/or shut down. They will have to determine where they have gone and make decisions about what they will do about them.

◆ *Staff to maintain customer relations, including implementing customer awareness.* Unless your clients understand the importance of the date problem, they will try to waylay your efforts in an attempt to get their immediate business requirements met. Make sure they know that the Year 2000 has a deadline that can't be extended and that they feel the impact if you're late in delivering a solution.

◆ *Support from executives and stockholders.* This is a cross-organizational project. Without senior backing, any efforts to coordinate "the fix" will fail. Competition for increasingly scarce resources and the desire to minimize the impact of making Year 2000 changes will delay decisions past the deadline.

◆ *Personnel to take emergency measures.* Once you decide to take action about this problem, you will have to implement practices to keep the problem from growing. Stop purchasing products that are not going to handle dates correctly. Make sure that new forms don't have 19 printed on them, and allow space for four-digit years.

Team Spirit

First and foremost, you will need a project manager. This should not be just a task assigned to the first person who volunteers. Project management is a profession that requires a distinct set of skills. Project managers sent us to the moon. They built the Boeing 777 and

Microsoft Windows 95. They coordinate, cajole, wheedle, and demand cooperation. They know how to manage people on important and stressful projects.

You will need several people to support your project manager. One large bank assembled a team consisting of the following players:

- *Applications development reps (five sites)*—to determine the impact of the Year 2000 on in-house-developed application systems, purchased computer applications, data purchased from other firms, and purchased software development tools.
- *Operations reps (two sites)*—to study the impact on systems administration software, hardware usage, data storage, work scheduling, and to define new resource requirements.
- *Technical programming representative*—to analyze the impact on operating systems software, compilers, utilities, process performance, and work on design of special tools to handle unique enterprise needs.
- *Database administration*—to investigate the use of dates in the data, handling by database management systems, storage of dates, and passing of date data between applications and to others outside the enterprise.
- *Production planners (two)*—to design high-level plans for repairing and replacing applications, systems software, computer hardware, and other equipment.
- *Forms development*—to review forms and forms design to determine the location of the printed century, the space to enter the century on forms, and replacement of forms throughout the enterprise.
- *Facilities engineer*—to locate embedded systems within the enterprise and determine what to do about them.
- *Purchasing*—to review all supplier contracts and ascertain the status of work of suppliers to fix the problem; change contracts to include stipulations that protect the enterprise.

- *Security*—to study the impact of Year 2000 on security and surveillance equipment and systems.
- *Legal*—to evaluate the impact on financial statements, develop contract wording, assess enterprise and management liability, and so on.
- *Audit*—to determine what is needed to meet regulatory changes, develop a process to monitor changes to data, and put a process in place to review the progress of the enterprise toward Year 2000 compliance.
- *Vendor reps from key computer providers (three)*—to coordinate ordering and replacement of hardware, systems software correction and updates, and provide advice on dealing with performance and capacity issues.

The bank organized this team loosely, with dotted-line authority assigned to the project manager. This team reflects the decentralized development and implementation of computer applications. It takes into account the need to coordinate change across a country where they have hundreds of offices. The presence of legal, audit, and purchasing reflects their concern not only for the dependency on others, but the effect they will have on others as they begin to fix their problem.

In the case of this team, the enterprise's chief executive officer was convinced of the need for such a team by *another* team that was commissioned to study the problem. The managing directors acted in unison to fund the project and commit resources.

Another organization put in place a smaller team, but a team nonetheless. It contained the following:

- *Technical coordinator*—to work with technical services and operations to obtain computing resources and coordinate changes to systems software.

- *Administrator*—to assemble and coordinate plans of each of the organizations within the enterprise so that human resources could be found and allocated to help them.
- *Personnel coordinator*—to work with organizations to acquire staff for the project from within and outside the enterprise.
- *Planner*—to develop detailed plans for changing computer software and data.
- *Technical liaison*—to work with systems programmers and database administrators on making changes and building tools and support programs.
- *Quality assurance*—to provide an independent assessment of the changes made and assess the risk of implementing those changes.
- *Process developer*—to develop a factorylike process for making changes to software and data, determine where improvements can be made, and find tools for automating routine tasks to free up skilled staff to do more complex work.

This team setup reflects limiting the scope to software and data repair and that this enterprise's business focus is on providing services. This is a centralized organization with all services located and directed out of a single site. In this situation, responsibility was spread to each of the functional areas, with applications development providing coordination and direction. The titles they assigned to team members were unique within the enterprise.

Of course, you can call the team members point guards or small forwards or quarterbacks or goalies. The point is, titles don't matter as long as the team accomplishes what you need it to. And make sure that they are the best people you can find.

To help you understand what you're up against, let's review the possible Y2K scenarios if you do nothing or do too little too late. Nearly every computing process is time-sensitive, including safes, phone systems, cooling and heating systems and thermostats, elevators, engines, security and sprinkler systems, video cameras, and much more. Dates enable scheduling processes, determine the sequence of events, record and control events, limit retention, set and limit values. In short, accurate dating *makes things happen.* Calendars were created to make life predictable and planning possible.

Just after "Auld Lang Syne" is sung on December 31, 1999, chances are that any computer system not 2000-ready will react in one of these two ways:

Dates will roll over to 01/01/00, but treat the year as 1900, the scenario that will result in expired credit cards, licenses, and the like, miscalculations of interest, mishandling of dated perishable products, and so on.

Or else, simply and without fanfare, your system will crash. Transactions won't be mishandled; they won't be handled at all: total shutdown.

Wakeup Call

People can't be involved in something they know nothing about, so one of the first steps is to create awareness of the Year 2000 situation throughout your enterprise. One organization realized the importance of an awareness program when it found its 2000 Team recruitment efforts going nowhere because of companywide insouciance. There are many reasons for this inability to recruit. One is that nobody wants to be associated with a job that is expected to terminate at a fixed point in time, especially one in which recruits will not be learning any new skills that will prepare them for the next job. The second is that the job is similar to picking up the trash. If you do it well, nobody notices; if you do it ineffectively, everybody notices. Chances of recognition and reward or promotion are seen as poor. In short, there is no perceived incentive to take on this job.

Some companies have already blazed the recruitment trail by including ongoing articles in their company newsletters or papers that highlight the Y2K team and the program; others have put out brochures signed by the CEO. Another program tied itself to an internal Employee Suggestion award program. At least one energetic person designed a screen saver, with some version of the warning, "The millennium is coming. This computer is not ready!"

Achieving visibility is important. Making sure that you have a team in place to exploit it is even more important. Some companies produce newsletters to bring the Y2K issue to the attention of employees to solicit coordinated effort. Unfortunately, newsletters often go unread. While work is going on to fix the problem, it has not yet reached the imperative level. It is not even clear to most that fixing the problem is important. This is not unusual. The more decentralized an enterprise becomes, the less able it will be to put together project teams with real authority to make things happen. The people from "corporate" have been declawed and defanged. In decentralized enterprises (federal and state governments fall into this category), each of the computing entities compete for resources and budget. A real leader will have to emerge to get these groups to work together.

One oblique way of getting the message across is to use an esti-mating survey. Questions like, "When will your application fail?" should be followed by others that help to determine the answer:

What is the longest forward dating used?
Do you enter dates in the future? If so how far?
How long do you expect data in the master file to be kept?
What is the oldest date stored in each master file?
What is the maximum retention cycle of any master file in the appli-
   cation?
How long does the system retain each transaction?
Are there regulatory or legal retention requirements?

Other awareness mechanisms include the following:

- Training programs for programmers and users to instruct them on standards, policies, and what to look for
- E-mail and voice mail to highlight costs and policy issues, provide instruction, and ensure cooperation
- Management briefings to kick off the 2000 recovery project, review budget issues, facilitate project progress and participation, and minimize business impact

One enterprising group within the U.S. Department of Defense has established a bulletin board on which employees can share questions, information, and experiences.

READING IS FUNDAMENTAL

Many organizations support their internal communications with information from outside sources. This book is one of several now being published that are aimed at awareness. Another good resource is the *Millennium Journal,* distributed by Data Dimensions and aimed primarily at computer managers. It is available on a World Wide Web site on the Internet (www.data-dimensions.com). Other consulting companies and many tool manufacturers have a presence on the Internet. Send one query over the Internet and you will have vendors beating down your doors (at least for a little while; when the pressure picks up, they will be waiting for the highest bidder to come to them). Another place for information is the "Year 2000 Information Center" located on the Internet at http://www.year2000.com.

This site will point you toward numerous vendors of tools and services and provide you with a forum for sharing problems and obtaining advice. You might even start looking there for employees. If you decide to join the Year 2000 forum, be aware that you may get buried in messages. E-mail is voluminous, and there are now over 200,000 accesses to this site per month.

If you're running out of time or just feeling lost, we suggest you use the frequently asked questions (FAQ), available from the Year 2000 Information Center, for assistance in sorting the wheat from the chaff.

You will find a similar special-interest group forming on Compu-Serve. Most hardware vendors and major software vendors are providing Year 2000 information about their products and what they are doing to solve their problems. And it wouldn't be a bad idea to subscribe to a couple of periodicals that address the Year 2000 issue. Try these:

Tick, Tick, Tick
2000AD, Inc.
P.O. Box 020538
Brooklyn, NY 11202-0012

ACM Software Engineering Notes and Communications of the ACM
ACM Press
11 West 42nd St.
New York, NY 10036
212-869-7440

Team Against Machine

It's game time, time to pit your Team 2000 against the millennium-defiant equipment in residence at your business. First let's dispel one myth: that only big old computers are susceptible to the Year 2000 date problem. You may think that your computer programs will work just fine because they were created last year or were put into a fancy new data management system that uses four-digit-year formats. Think again.

Take this test: Find your PC's internal or system clock. On a PC running DOS, you can do this by typing DATE. Change the date to December 31, 1999. Change the time by setting TIME to 11:58 P.M. Then turn off the computer and wait three minutes. When you turn it back on, does it read January 1, 2000? If so, congratulations. Your hardware would seem to be okay.

Some Apple Macintoshes, Gateway 2000 PCs, recently manufactured IBM PCs, PCs with OS/2 WARP, Windows 95/NT, and a few others will pass this test. (However, you still need to check your own spreadsheets and make sure you're using software that handles two-digit years correctly.) Most of you undoubtedly found some bizarre number, possibly January 4, 1980. The simple explanation is that the computer's internal clock is set using counters from a previously selected date. These counters have only so many digits and can hold only so many seconds. When they are full, they reset themselves back to the original date.

Of course, you're going to have to check all your programs, too. Microsoft's position is that all programs written prior to 1997 should be replaced beginning in 1998 with software written for the latest release of Windows. These products will use the operating system clock rather than the hardware clock. This will certainly mean that any software you are dependent on today may not work well with operating systems developed in the near future.

PC INVENTORY

Some PC computer manufacturers are attempting to resolve this problem. We'll use IBM to illustrate the point, which is that there are a lot of PC products, and it will take someone trained to identify which ones you have and then to determine what it will take to fix them. The inventory will take a lot of time, except for the smallest businesses, especially to do it right. You will be locating job streams, databases, files, applications, and shared code. (You will need this information later.)

According to an IBM publication titled "The Year 2000 and 2-Digit Dates: A Guide for Planning and Implementation," all new models of IBM PCs shipped in 1996 and later will automatically update the century. They have confirmed that the following older models of PC will be affected by date problems:

- All XT286, all ATs, all PS/1s, all PS/2s, all PS/55s.
- All Aptivas before 1996.
- Most 2144 systems.
- Most 2168 systems, although they will update the century byte automatically after you install the flash BIOS available from IBM's Bulletin Board service.
- Commercial desktop PC systems such as the PS/V (models 2405/2410), the PS/V Vision (model 2408), the PS/V Entry (model 2406), the PS/V MASTER (model 2411), the PC 750 (model 6885), the PC 330 (model 6571), and so forth must have the century byte set manually.

Check with IBM if you discover you have any of its PC hardware in house.

The hardware timers on RS/6000 servers, as well as personal systems using PowerPC technology, will not be affected by the turning of the millennium, but it's probably a good idea to test them anyway. IBM PC servers introduced in 1996 will handle the century rollover automatically, which says all you need to know about those introduced prior to that date.

Some current and earlier IBM PCs will handle the change quite well, but testing should be conducted to determine which ones they are. The tests involve taking the PC off any network it might be attached to and then running the test given earlier, where the date is set to just prior to the rollover to the Year 2000—12:59:00 on December 31, 1999—and then the PC is turned off for a couple of minutes. Check the date on the system clock and the clock in the operating system to see what date, day, and time appear. They should register as a Saturday, a few minutes after 12 A.M. on January 1, 2000. Remember to do full backups of all your systems before you start date testing.

Commands and utilities are available to help some models weather the changeover. If you are running DOS, which is unlikely at that date, it is possible to enter the correct date using the DATE command. Contact IBM to find out which models need help, and which might have to be abandoned.

You may (probably) have computers from another manufacturer—clones. If so, find out if the manufacturer has a Year 2000 plan in place. If it doesn't—which is usually the case—at least it is better to know now than to be "surprised" later.

Hardware

To determine your PC status, start by taking an inventory. It will probably take from 10 to 15 minutes to register each PC. Collect the following information:

Manufacturer
Model
BIOS manufacturer
BIOS version number

The last two pieces of information should appear when the computer starts up. Even if you find that the manufacturer of your machines is no longer in business, you may still be able to determine

whether the PC is 2000-vulnerable by contacting the BIOS manufacturer. And remember, having bought computers in 1996 or later does
not guarantee they are 2000-ready! They may have been built using a
BIOS that was manufactured much earlier.

Software

Don't stop at the hardware. You also need to know how many software program updates you will have to buy. PC software is not
exempt from the issue of old release versus the century-compliant
release. Older DOS releases and even some Windows versions of
popular software such as Sidekick, Quicken, Excel, and Lotus 1-2-3
do not all handle dates in 2000 in the same way. These inconsistencies
will cause problems. Older programs and the Windows 3.x calendar
function do not handle the century rollover properly, and date problems abound in interpackage data sharing because dates are assumed
to be prefixed by either 19 or 20.

Fortunately, software packages are available to help you complete
your software inventory. Greenwich Mean Time Inc. (56 Oyster
Quay, Port Solent, Portsmouth, Hampshire, UK P06 4TE) provides a
package to do this inventory. (Their URL is www.gmt.2000.com.)
The following are some generic steps that will help you to complete
this inventory.

1. Task every organization with completing a PC inventory.
2. The inventory should contain the following information:

   - Whether the PC is a client, server, or stand-alone model
   - Model number
   - Processor type (e.g., Intel 486 100 MHz)
   - BIOS date
   - Software operating system and version number
   - Vendor packages loaded on the hard drive (product name,
     vendor, version)

- Internally developed software packages
- All spreadsheets that are used routinely
- All databases that are used routinely
- LAN ID number and address; name of LAN

3. Consolidate the list in a database or spreadsheet.

This information will enable you to determine licenses that need upgrades and training requirements. The processor type will tell you whether you are faced with hardware replacement. Vendor packages and versions will tell you how many and which products have to be upgraded. Greenwich Mean Time's Check 2000 also provides Year 2000 compliancy information on the products it inventories.

Don't be surprised to discover that many of your PCs are running software with duplicate serial numbers. Often, people reload with the first set of disks at hand. Any system or program can be affected if it uses only two digits for the year. Old habits die hard: Recently developed desktop software often has the same problem because it is easier for programmers to reuse old chunks of code and plug them in than to write each program from scratch.

And be aware that you may experience trouble well in advance of the year 2000, if you haven't already. Application programs working with such time-sensitive data are likely to produce incorrect results today.

Ashes to Ashes, DOS to Dust

Microsoft is taking steps to correct date problems. The program interfaces for Windows 95 and Windows NT are capable of storing dates for 119 years, starting from 1980, so applications that rely on those formats will work until 2099. Although these particular Microsoft operating systems handle dates well into the next century, mainframe operating system dates historically have not. Programs designed to run in these environments (as well as OS/2, UNIX, and Mac) generally use the operating system clock and not the computer clock. If you are running DOS, you are more likely to find problems with dates.

Many computers can't tell the difference between a day in 1905 and one in 2005 with a two-digit-year date format. The updated Microsoft products that assume the year from two-digit dates will be updated in 1997 to make it easier for the computer to assume a 2000-based year. As a result, Microsoft recommends that by the end of the century all PC software be upgraded to versions from 1997 and beyond. (Is that your checkbook you hear whimpering?)

According to a company paper on the implications of the Year 2000, Microsoft warns developers, including those using macrolanguages or building custom databases using products like Microsoft Access, to use date formats that accommodate the transition to the year 2000. Recommendations include the following:

1. Use the operating system's runtime library's date format as much as possible.
2. Use long dates (four-digit years) rather than short ones whenever creating a custom application.
3. Buy all new hardware and software and hope for the best.

Some Microsoft Windows systems don't use the same 32-bit platform as Windows 95 or Windows NT. Windows for Workgroups 3.11, Windows 3.1, and any earlier versions still in use come to mind. The following table shows Microsoft's current products and the life expectancy of the date formats for each. Unless otherwise noted, the products rely on the system-supplied date formats. As you can see, some of these products won't make it much past the year 2000 before running into problems. This does not include the many products that won't make it there at all, so you probably should examine

all your current Microsoft programs with the same diligence that you
do the rest of your software portfolio.

Product Name	Date Limit	Date Format
Microsoft Access 95 assumed date	1999	assumed 'yy' dates
Microsoft Access 95 explicit date	9999	long dates (yyyy)
Microsoft Access (next major version)	2039	assumed 'yy' dates
Microsoft Excel 95	2019	assumed 'yy' dates
Microsoft Excel 95	2078	long dates
Microsoft Excel (next major version)	2029	assumed 'yy' dates
Microsoft Excel (next major version)	9999	long dates
Microsoft Project 95 (and older versions)	2049	32 bits
Microsoft SQL Serve	9999	'datetime'
MS-DOS file system (FAT16)	2108	16 bits
Visual C++ (4.x) runtime library	2036	32 bits
Visual FoxPro	9999	long dates
Windows 3.x file system (FAT16)	2108	16 bits
Windows 95 file system (FAT16)	2108	16 bits
Windows 95 file system (FAT32)	2108	32 bits
Windows 95 runtime library (WIN32)	2099	16 bits
Windows for Workgroups (FAT16)	2108	16 bits
Windows NT file system (FAT16)	2108	16 bits
Windows NT file system (NTFS)	future	64 bits centuries
Windows NT runtime library (WIN32)	2099	16 bits

Courtesy of Microsoft and available via the Internet.

Of course, this table assumes that the owner of the PC has up-to-
date software, up-to-date hardware, and no trouble with the BIOS
clock. Smart PC owners will not make these assumptions, but will
check for themselves.

DOS is expected to die, even though a new version will be
released. Remember, all Windows programs should be replaced after
the WIN 97 release. Windows 3.x will also probably disappear. Ven-

dors do not like to spend money providing fixes for old operation systems.

Many organizations will have to update software and hardware for the simple reason that combined changes are much harder to implement successfully. And because most information departments do not control PCs, networks, and user programs, many end users will use the change to introduce Windows 95 with all the attendant problems for the central organization.

Chapter Three

Avoiding Future Shock

These days, the Social Security Administration seems anything but secure, as government spending threatens its very existence. It may then seem surprising that the SSA has been at the forefront of efforts to deal with the Year 2000 problem, working since 1989 to rewrite its code to be 2000-ready. But even with an 11-year head start, it will take the Social Security Administration until 1998 to complete its task, a clear indication of the enormity of this problem.

Action Hero

The point is, you need to take action quickly but methodically, because seat-of-the-pants tactics will result in wasted effort. Before you take on the biggest project of your life, be sure you are fore-armed with a plan. Your ability to correct the Y2K problem will depend upon the following:

- Understanding that the scope of the problem encompasses more than computers.

- Estimating what it will cost to fix and finding the money to do so.
- Identifying and contacting your vendors and suppliers to find out their awareness/readiness.
- Setting up a project team.
- Building awareness to obtain cooperation.
- Inventorying your computers—determining where and how old they are and what is running on them. Which are your critical systems? Which will be impacted first by threshold dates? In what sequence will changes have to be made so that you can keep your enterprise up and running?

A typical enterprise software portfolio includes all systems that manage the products and/or services provided by the company. It typically includes human resource systems, e-mail, accounts payable, accounts receivable, actuarial programs, operating systems, and document imaging and/or scanning programs, as well as some word processing programs, spreadsheets, and databases—and don't forget that little envelope-printing program the mailroom clerk uses because he or she doesn't like the company-supplied one very much.

At this juncture, you should have your enterprise team in place, and all of them should be 2000-aware. Now it's time to assess your level of dependency on others—who, by the way, may be in deeper trouble than you.

THE DANGERS OF CODEPENDENCY

Get out the list you made of all your suppliers and vendors. It is time to determine what recourse you have and what response you can expect from them. Ask yourself the following questions:

- Do your contracts entitle you to fixes?
- Are there performance guarantees?

- Will your suppliers or vendors be willing and/or able to meet those terms?
- If the provider is able to perform, but with some delays, what is the risk to your business if you can't meet commitments for days or weeks? Can you stay in business if suppliers can't operate for a given period—especially if they are your sole source? You might want to look into finding alternate sources, workarounds, or creating a stock pile in case of emergency.
- If your ability to perform is diminished by supplier/vendor breakdown, how will this affect your customers, employees, retirees, and your ability to meet regulatory requirements?

Answering these questions will put you in a proactive position. True, you still won't be able to control some of these elements, but knowing the probability of their occurrence will give you a leg up in dealing with them.

One of the first things you can do is contain the problem to the present: Make sure all your future contracts include statements to relieve you of responsibility should you be unable to perform because of the breakdown of your supply chain or delivery mechanism. This is especially important for service providers.

DEPENDENT AND UNSUPPORTED

Conducting your hardware and software inventory probably seemed like opening Pandora's box. You no doubt found one or more of these nasty surprises:

- You have programs running no one seems to know anything about.
- Most applications pass data across system boundaries.
- There is no clear ownership of much of the data.
- Many programs being run are not supported by in-house staff.

- Many programs can't be easily associated because naming standards are not enforced.
- Source code is missing.
- There is a dearth of tools that enable you to track things.
- Some programs, tools, and utilities were purchased from a vendor no longer in business; some products were sold; or you've let maintenance contracts lapse.
- You may be running vendor software illegally. Certain software may be licensed to a specific computer only; and pricing schedules may be different for certain computer processor sizes. Many organizations overlook these contract points when they acquire new equipment.

MULTILINGUAL MADNESS

Your software survey team will also need to inventory the many different versions of the various products and programming languages used by the company. As mentioned earlier, you may uncover code written in languages that essentially are dead—a serious problem if no one on the current staff knows the language or the product is no longer sold. Many of these have date problems that can't be fixed, and no conversion option exists to translate them to another language.

Other programs you unearth may have been written in languages that, while extant, are so old and have been running untouched for so long that the program converting them to machine-understandable form (a compiler) is no longer available. One of the most common languages used in business applications is COBOL, which comes in about 30 different versions. Some companies have several different versions of COBOL on the same computer at the same time, each of which reacts to the Year 2000 in different, though equally ugly, ways.

AN ARM AND A LEG

Pull out your hardware survey and put it on top of the pile. Did you identify which outdated machines you are relying on and which version of the operating system they are running on? Determine whether it can process dates past December 31, 1999, without going into red alert. If it can't, it may be time to place an equipment order. Find out if there are conversion programs to move your applications. And don't forget to make sure that the new software will be Year 2000–compliant. You probably will want to order extra data storage, too, because conversions and the update and testing processes are bound to eat it up more quickly.

Using the inventory you compiled in the previous chapter, you will next estimate the cost. At the same time you are doing this, try also to determine how much time it's going to take to fix and test everything. You can purchase scanning programs to look for the incidence of dates in your code and estimating packages that will forecast the staffing requirements, duration, and cost of making the code changes.

You will have to take the time to acquire these products, learn how to use them, and then get set up to run them. Most consulting companies will offer services and tools to provide this information more efficiently than you can.

Some organizations prefer to skip this step, and they calculate a simple amount advocated by some consulting organizations. At various times, we've seen the amounts $.60, $1.00, $1.10, and $1.50 applied to the *total* number of code lines in your inventory—not just the number of lines to be changed.

The problem with using these amounts is that they are broad-stroke industry averages that may have little application in your environment. If you have missing source code, a lot of real-time processing code, and code using obsolete compilers, expect your costs to be much higher. If much or most of your code has been purchased from vendors who are working on making their products compliant, expect your costs to be lower.

Many of these industry estimates are based on work done by enterprises that have been successful in managing their own application conversions. They have typically been working on the problem for four to six years. Their costs are sometimes "best guesses" because other work (e.g., upgrading compilers or moving to new databases) is being performed simultaneously. There has yet to be a scientific study of the true cost of performing the Year 2000 changes.

TROUBLE ON THE HORIZON

The next element that you will want to determine is the *event horizon*. This is a term used by consultants to express the point in time when applications will cease to function correctly or cease to function at all. The concept of the event horizon is critical in developing a plan to resolve the Year 2000 problem. You must first determine the earliest potential failure date and make sure the application is converted or replaced before that time. The event horizon for an application is fairly easy to calculate:

- Determine how far into the future stored files are dated.
- Identify the oldest dates in the application.

Knowing the event horizon and the duration of the project will tell you if there is enough time to make the change. Let's say you are a magazine publisher and you sell two-year subscriptions. You know that you will not be able to enter two-year subscriptions without changing your systems after January 1, 1998. In fact, you know that you will start entering subscriptions by October that expire in 2000 because you are planning a Christmas offer. Your event horizon is therefore October 1, 1997. The estimates indicate that, based on the factors you have entered, you should have five people working on the package for eight months. This means that in order to get the job done by October the process must start on February 1, 1997. If you discover this in March 1997, you are already behind. You will have to decide among the options of hiring more people, postponing the Christmas offer until December, or dropping two-year subscriptions from the Christmas offer.

For this example, we'll assume you decide to go ahead. You will quickly find that the billing system has become more complicated because it uses the expiration date in the subscription system. Thus it has to be changed in time to produce the bills that go along with the two-year subscriptions. That system, however, may not be required to be compliant until the magazines are shipped. If the magazines are shipped a month ahead, in December, that is the event horizon for the billing system. If the magazine is bimonthly, the event horizon is in November. That means you'll have to get both systems done at the same time to meet the Christmas offering; or you can "patch" the billing system to handle the offering and make any other changes later, which means you are going into the same system twice. That will require more work because you will have to retest. (Yes, this is complicated; welcome to Year 2000 project planning.)

With your event horizon in hand, your next concern is how much time it will take to convert or replace the system.

SAND THROUGH THE HOURGLASS

If you, like many, will not have enough time to make all your systems 2000-compliant, you will have to make the following decisions:

- Which systems are mission-critical; that is, which must be up and running to keep your company alive?
- Which systems can make the transition without affecting your business?

♦ Which ones will have to be abandoned because you won't have time to change them?

Only you can decide which systems and functions are the most important to your company. Pareto's rule applies here, because 80 percent of your benefit is derived from 20 percent of your applications.

PEOPLE WHO NEED PEOPLE

Now determine your staff and computer resources. Previously, we mentioned the project planning and coordinating teams, which are part of the corporate date solution. Here we're talking about those who actually get into the code or the equipment. Fortune 100 corporations may need hundreds or thousands of employees working on the problem to get it fixed in time. If, say, you have a staff of 10 and have three years left, then you have 30 years' worth of effort to allocate to this project. If the survey says you will need 45 years' worth of effort, some systems will have to fend for themselves, by which we mean that they will have to be run without attention. In fact, someone on the user side will have to check constantly to verify that these systems are running correctly; if a problem occurs, the staff will have to request a fix. But that is far preferable to having the whole enterprise go down. And now's the time to get tough, because the sooner you decide which systems must be fixed, the greater your chances of delivering them on time.

Triage: Computer Style

You should come away from the exercises in the previous sections with the knowledge of which parts of your company are the most important and, thus, valuable. (If you're tempted to think the answer's obvious, remember that threats to normal business processes have a way of casting operating assumptions in a whole new light.) Once you determine which systems you have, what needs to be fixed, and the resources you have with which to fix them, you are able to perform triage—computer style.

Triage is used mainly in battlefield situations where the casualties outnumber the available medical resources. At such times, resources have to be allocated to victims according to a system of priorities designed to maximize the number of survivors. Setting these types of priorities involves making some difficult decisions.

Applied to the Year 2000 situation, this concept requires slight modification. We're not trying to save the individual systems; we're trying to save the organization relying on those systems.

1. We first identify mission-critical systems: those systems that we've pointed to every time we've had to justify our existence. Mission-critical systems are a handful of applications supplying the motivating force behind the business.

2. The next group of applications are those we could live without for awhile, and perhaps forever. Their loss would affect our ability to conduct business . . . but we could continue shipping product and providing basic services, however slowly, expensively, and inefficiently.

3. Finally, identify those systems you run, but don't really need and wouldn't really miss. At first you might respond, "We need everything we run! Otherwise we wouldn't be running it!" My response is that Pareto's rule likely applies to computer systems more than to any other human endeavor. Looked at from the hind end, 80 percent of what you do generates less than 20 percent of the benefit. And it's going to get worse.

LOOKING OUT FOR #1

Needless to say, we're going to ignore everything but the first group. Simply put, if you don't have the resources to save everything, what you do have must be focused on getting those mission-critical systems operational when the ball drops. Doing anything else is poor project management and judgment.

This process is difficult to automate, although some productivity tools are available to help speed it up. The final result of this resource-intensive task is a specification for change that you can then use to implement the actual changes in codes and files in the next stages.

Reducing the Options

The reality is, even mission-critical systems contain more than they need. We were once told there are 50,000 ways to purchase an airline ticket: using discounts, charter programs, group rates; staying over Saturday; bringing your own food, bringing food for the pilot; flying on a day that doesn't have a Y in it . . . well, you get the picture. Are all these options necessary? Not when it comes down to choosing between having a system with everything on it or no system at all.

You will have to make tough decisions if you intend to greet 2000 with a smile. You may have to revert to bare-bones programming in order to survive. (Naturally, not all systems can be slimmed down without involving an entire rewrite. And this is *not* the time for that.) Systems that obviously have to be fixed are those involved with product or service delivery (manufacturing, shipping/receiving, inventory, bill of materials, etc.), selling, and billing for the product or services. Accounting systems that handle crediting for payments, paying for services (including payroll), and general ledger are also essential.

The typical event horizon for a budgeting system is five years. This unfortunately is no longer feasible, since 2000 is little more than three years away. Some credit card companies that renew clients for a period of four years have already discovered their systems will not accept dates past 1999. The question is, will your applications continue to operate properly for 1999, 2000, and 2001? An application that processes future dates may already have an undiscovered failure (this is called a *soft* or *hidden* failure).

Several types of hidden failures occur. The following are representative.

- A transaction is created for the Year 2000 and filed. The system interprets the date as 1900 and stores the record under that date. Queries to find the records for Year 2000 return no responses. Queries for records written in 1900 are rejected because the validation routine catches it. The user thinks the transaction is lost and reenters it. Only a physical search of the database can locate the record. In some cases, the normal processes continue showing the correct number of records and processing against the transaction as if it were open and normal.
- A transaction is processed as dated in 1900. An interest calculation is performed, but the field is not large enough to hold the value, so the amount is truncated. The values may be larger or smaller than they should be, but because everything appears to be working, this error is not recognized until monthly or quarterly summaries are generated.
- A transaction is processed as dated in Year 2000 and everything appears normal. During the month, the number-of-days calculation is performed on an overdue payment routine. It looks at only the last two digits of the date, indicates that the account is overdue, and issues an overdue notice. The calculation of the overdue amount uses a different routine and prints zero amount overdue. A dunning notice is sent to the customer.

After several increasingly demanding dunning notices are sent, the angry customer calls. There is no record of a problem, so the call is dismissed. The customer keeps getting the notices, and finally bill collectors are given the account. They bring the problem to the attention of accounts receivable, but by that time the client has terminated his or her account.

Beg, Borrow, Steal

We don't really recommend that you beg, borrow, or steal to keep your systems up and running into 2000; our recommendation is to *buy, trade up,* or *transform.* Obviously, the most important consideration is getting all your changes done on time, so use whatever will work for you and your company.

BUY

Those systems (accounting systems come to mind) you determine to be candidates for reduction may be eligible for help from a commercial "diet" plan. If you realize that, on your own, you can't fix your entire system in time, perhaps you should consider an off-the-shelf product. Dun and Bradstreet and Great Plains Software both have announced their products will be Year 2000–compliant. Perhaps they or some other vendors offer a way out.

But don't expect such packages to meet 100 percent of your requirements. Only custom software can do that, though not as well as you would hope. However, you can usually adapt the business to fit the package. Keep in mind that each change you make to the packaged software will increase the installation time.

TRADE UP

Another alternative is to trade in your application for a better model. Many programs are still in place because they work. They may be old; they may be ugly; but they're paid for. And some enterprises run more than one version of the programs because one department or division wanted features another did not. Now's the time to standardize. It will save time. Replace an older version with the latest version—but be sure to find out if it's 2000-compliant before you do so.

Resist, though, the temptation you may feel with this option to throw the old application into the trash, then spend too much valuable time developing a new in-house version complete with bells and whistles. Remember, time is running short. Your priority now is to be ready for the Year 2000. A new and glorious program would be great, but not at the expense of company survival. You don't have time for everyone to learn a new system. If you'd started on this project five years ago, it might have been possible, but you're way too close to the deadline to risk the company on it now.

TRANSFORM

And then there's *transform*. The focus of this effort is to coax your programs past the Year 2000 using a number of different methods that will enable them to perform their normal functions. Automated tools can help your programmers find most of the dates, though they will still have to hunt for some hidden ones. Other tools can help them change the hidden dates so the program can deal with the Year 2000, though they will have to use other techniques as well.

Only you can decide whether or not to do all this in-house, hire some of it out, or hire all of it out. Some companies prefer not to have others know their business, while others feel that they are better off concentrating on their products or services, letting the computer experts handle the technological problems.

But be aware, if you decide to seek outside help, you will run into computer contractors who promise you the proverbial moon. According to research done by Capers Jones, a pioneer in software measurement, the likelihood of any programming effort being delivered on time is less than 62 percent. When Jones analyzed large projects involving more than 12.5 million lines of code, the percentage plummeted to less than 14 percent. If you hire a contractor, examine his or her delivery record, especially on large projects.

CALLING IN THE CAVALRY

If and when you decide to hire outside help, your first order of business, as just mentioned, is to ascertain their track record. Then find out if they can do the following:

- Meet the deadline of January 1, 2000.
- Work with internal and external interfaces.
- Insert the code changes for both procedural and data structure. (Not only will they have to change nearly all your procedures, but also the way your company stores the information.)
- Perform file and database conversions. (Being able to access information compiled from past years may be important.)
- Coordinate internal and external staff. Helping people work well together under these circumstances is going to be difficult, but necessary.
- Commit to an extensive work effort, which could span years.
- Perform phased implementations. Changing over all at once could easily throw things into chaos.
- Plan, track, and control all programs in an organization.

Secondary functions you may want or expect an outside service to perform include the following:

- Updating the language your computer uses and standardizing it so all of your programs speak one language.
- Expanding financial fields or implementing other changes in how your company stores information.
- Eliminating dead code, which will give you more computer space to work with.
- Rationalizing data names—if you have to examine your system again in the future, you will want to be able to figure out what you've got.
- Reversing engineering of data structures and procedure code into a central repository—giving future managers and workers necessary information they'll need the next time something goes wrong.
- Upgrading applications and user documentation.
- Adding tools to enable you to determine how well your programs are working, how well the conversion progress is going, and to make testing easier.

These extras should be considered only if they will not delay the delivery of the Year 2000–ready product.

In Charge of the Light Brigade

These lists may have encouraged you to believe that someone is going to save you and your company from ruin. And that may be so, but only if you stay involved, which means you have to know how to manage any outside help you hire. Do not let them manage you.

The planning activities outlined in this chapter will give you the best chance for success in the Year 2000. You will tackle only meaningful work. You will have a team in place to do the work. You will have the cooperation and support of both management and the rest of the company. Are you ready to run?

Chapter Four

Ready to Run

The planning activities outlined so far are the first steps toward solving the Year 2000 problem. To reiterate: You will tackle only meaningful work. You will put a team in place to do the work and enlist the cooperation and support of both executive management and other departments. While you are engaged in these activities, your computer people should be taking other actions, defined in this chapter, which will lead you through the steps involved in creating a process. This is not a trivial or a simple activity. It involves defining and reducing the work to a routine so that it may be completed as expeditiously as possible, with as much automation as can be brought to bear.

The process building activities involve the following:

1. Setting standards
2. Defining a working update process
3. Creating a controlled change environment
4. Establishing a testing environment
5. Selecting tools
6. Choosing and executing a process pilot

Setting Standards

Smart businesspeople realize that creating standards is a way to avoid having to make the same decisions over and over again. In addressing the Year 2000 problem, some standards are obvious, and therefore easy to set:

- Buy only products that are Year 2000–compliant.
- Design software programs so that they are Year 2000–compliant.
- Define Year 2000 compliance (unfortunately no one definition has yet found global acceptance).
- Define minimum requirements for date testing prior to Year 2000 changes. (Remember, many programs don't process dates correctly.)
- Define minimum requirements for Year 2000 testing.

The one standards decision that often causes dissension is whether to standardize on two-digit or four-digit years. The first option usually is greeted with dismay by noncomputing people. After all, isn't that the problem? No. The problem is not in using a two-digit year designation; the problem is that the *programs* were not designed to use two-digit years across millennium boundaries. In the first chapter, we suggested this was a *design* problem.

The decision to standardize on four-digit versus two-digit years is actually very simple. *Use the one that will get you standardized the fastest with the least risk.* That said, however, the most cost-effective solution over the long term *is* to move to four digits. This will mean fewer program design changes, but it will require data changes. Making changes to handle two-digit years means the reverse. Thus, the question of which to do depends on the data and the processing required to process two-digit-year data in a four-digit environment.

Suffice it to say that every organization currently engaged in the Year 2000 redesign has to take one path or the other and compromise when necessary. Our advice is to set the standard for the long term and then define the rules for doing things in the short term. Employ four-digit years whenever and wherever possible. Where the cost of employing four-digit years is prohibitive or the time required to implement the data changes is threatened by an event horizon, use two-digit years.

YEAR 2000–COMPLIANT

Discussions of the Year 2000 computer problem invariably raise the concept of Year 2000–compliant or –compatible applications. And as usual with concepts, their definitions vary depending on the circumstances of implementation. It doesn't matter what anyone else thinks 2000–compliant means. It is only necessary that you and your organization agree on a working definition before you begin implementing a change process.

Your first attempt at a definition might be based on the obvious assertion that if all years were represented as four digits, then applications would be Year 2000–compliant. It's tempting to declare that any application using fewer than four digits to represent the year be deemed incompatible. While that has a certain simplicity and elegance, you'll quickly find it's too strict a definition, mainly because the standard MMDDYY (MM being the space allocated for two numbers representing the month, DD for day, and YY for year) is almost universal. Some organizations have taken steps to standardize on YYMMDD or YYYYMMDD just because it is less ambiguous to have a single format.

A much simpler definition, sidestepping the entire technical coding requirements debate, is to say that if an application is working correctly today and will continue to work correctly during and following the Year 2000, it is compliant. Some organizations have bounded the period, which must be considered. GTE, for example, looks at the range of dates from January 1, 1900 to December 31, 2050 as being the key dates. They specifically note that all years divided evenly by 4, except for 1900, must be correctly handled as leap years.

The challenge is to prove that a program is compliant according to this definition, because it is impossible to test today's complex applications to the point of determining that they are 100 percent error-free. Part of the problem is that many applications have become so complex that nobody really knows what the program is doing, or if it is doing it correctly.

An all too common occurrence of people delving into their code to determine what to fix is uncovering instances of date calculations that have been performed incorrectly for years—calculations that have been accepted as correct by management, users, and clients. Consequently, you may have to backtrack and rectify errors of past years. Alternatively, you may decide to sustain that error but to make sure that it works correctly from now on. This means getting the program to ignore those past incorrect calculations, while performing all future ones correctly.

It is alarming to realize that in the past, testing applications against the Year 2000 has been specifically and deliberately avoided. Why? Because programmers and managers knew that if they tested their accounting applications, for example, against a year with a value of 00, the program would fail.

The consequence of this is that most people have very little experience with these types of temporal tests. Testing dates involves thinking about the possibility of miscalculation or faulty logic. Test cases must involve testing for the correct rollover of dates. Dates frequently tested to assess millennium compliance include 1998-12-31, 1999-09-09, 1999-12-31, 2000-01-01, 2000-02-28, 2000-02-29, 2000-03-01, 2000-12-31, 2001-01-01, 2027-12-31. Of these, there are two that most people find unusual: 1999-09-09 is a legitimate date, but it can be handled incorrectly by programs that test for 9s only; 2027-12-31 represents the limits of many computers' date storage capacity and often rolls over the storage buffers, giving an invalid result. To completely test the applications, it is necessary to test the handling of invalid dates. Many have found their applications sailing right past 1900-02-29, 1999-99-99, 2000-00-00, 2001-02-29, 2001-02-30, and 2100-02-29 as if they were perfectly legitimate dates. Testing to see if it is possible to break the system is as important as testing to see if it works correctly.

In addition, to properly test for the Year 2000 you have to time-warp all of your systems, hardware, and software into the future, which is difficult to do when many of the underlying applications such as the operating systems themselves are not yet ready to be tested in this manner. The only real test of the Year 2000 will come on January 1, 2000 as everything ticks over into the new year, for real, and forever. Finding yourself in situations where your passwords or software license have expired when you move the system date forward could be irksome, and may cause time-consuming work-arounds.

This brings us back full circle to how we go about defining millennium compliance. The following definition for *century compliance* was adopted by the Bank of Boston:

- Date fields must have a two-character century field (i.e., CCYY); and processing logic is sound.
- Data input specifies valid century.
- Hard-coding in century fields and date fields has been removed.
- Applications will interface with all date data that is imported or exported.
- Date validation routines must include century.
- No null values in the field converted to 00.

- No date fields used for other than date purposes (i.e., date used as a logical switch).
- There is a legitimate plan to retire or replace the application prior to the event horizon.

GTE has taken a different approach. Its compliance rules are as follows:

- No value of current date will cause interruptions in desired operation.
- All manipulations of time-related data (dates, durations, days of week, etc.) will produce desired results for all valid date values within the application domain.
- Date elements in interfaces and data storage permit specifying century to eliminate date ambiguity.
- All software maintained by and for GTE may contain literals or constants for dates unless required to capture specific business rules.
- Date fields must be initialized with either all zeros or null values (the latter as defined by the development facilities such as the compiler).
- Applications may not use special date values as logical flags.
- For any date element represented without a century, the correct century is unambiguous for all manipulations involving that element.
- All developed and third-party software must permit the use of date formats that explicitly specify century according to ANSI X3.30 in all data stored or transmitted, unless there is a superior application standard or convention.
- Third-party products must permit formatting data with explicit century in the user interface.
- All developed applications using third-party products must always explicitly supply century and never rely on those products' default value for century.

- Developed and third-party software may imply century in the user interface format, YYMMDD or YYJJJ (as specified in ANSI X3.30).
- In storing or transmitting date data, some applications must conform to domain-specific standards whose requirements for dates may supersede ANSI X3.30, as appropriate.

These standards reflect the possibility of standards or custom that allows or requires date definitions not fully compliant with ANSI X3.30. Exceptions defined even allow for certain editing masks to be used as deemed necessary by standard or custom. Obviously, these expectations are finding their way into contracts for third-party software. Sometimes, the wording of the contract is very simple, requiring the vendor to define the testing and meet the obligation, something to the effect of, "Process all dates between 1900 and 2100 without error or opportunity for ambiguity." The point, lest it be missed, is that you not only have to protect your organization against third-party practices, but also against its own.

Creating an Update Process

Nothing will be more important to you in the update process than *creating the update process*. By doing so, you can find out a number of things:

- What obstacles are being encountered?
- What manual tasks are required?
- What is needed before the output can be passed?
- Where do components need to be kept while being worked on?
- Where is the input to a process exceeding its capacity?
- When does each activity need to begin?
- Who needs to be involved?

You also need to create an *awareness* of the process. Rather than project managers, you will need process managers—people who not only look at schedules, but also at what determines those schedules. This is not an easy transition for experienced computing people to make. That's why the best process managers often come from outside. You need to find someone who always asks, "Why?" Put such a person on your update team. Of course, if you can find a computer person who can do that, even better. He or she might be able to find a solution at the same time.

Creating a Controlled Change Environment

There are two significant components of this activity. The first requires taking the inventory we already discussed and building a tracking mechanism. The second is to establish a software change control process. Both steps are essential. Many computer programs are shared by applications; thus it is necessary to track progress so that you know what has been done and what has not. It is also important to know this before changes are made so that alterations made to such programs do not accidentally affect another program. It is also not uncommon for millennium update changes to be made in parallel with other production changes, requiring a merger of the two changes prior to reintroducing the software to the production environment.

Planning and Tracking

To do this, you need to find out what you have on your computers, what needs to be changed, and what you are going to change. Ideally, this should be done at the same time you are establishing the inven-

tory as discussed in Chapter 1 and doing the scheduling as suggested
in Chapter 3. The best place to put this inventory is on a computer. If
your environment is not terribly complex, containing lots of internally developed programs and time-dependent processing, it does
not have to be a fancy process. Many organizations have done very
well with a PC-based spreadsheet or database application.

If your environment is complex, you will want to track a lot of
different items. Programs share tables, file definitions, and common
processing modules. Programs are related to data. Programs and data
are related to computer job streams or process sequences. It will be
helpful if you know, when you schedule one program to be changed,
which data or definitional code will have to be changed at the same
time and which other production processing actions are affected.
Some of these changes will be affected by, or affect, vendor products—application packages and/or systems software. Large enterprises put this component planning/tracking tool on their biggest
computers to make the information available to the whole team
rather than a single administrative person.

There are software products available from vendors (we explore
buying vendor tools in Chapter 8) that do this kind of component
relationship mapping, but they often are limited to a single platform
and do not capture all component relationships such as the systems
software components. A good Year 2000 planning/tracking tool not
only keeps track of application software, but also of vendor software,
external data files, systems software, and hardware. The best of them
have been custom-built by the enterprise or, under contract, by consulting organizations that specialize in large-scale conversion projects. These, unfortunately, are not for sale. Commercially available
relationship mapping tools will give the moderate to large organization a good footing.

You must give the process team the resources it needs. This
requires setting up a documentation system so you know exactly
which component changes are going to be made, when they're going

to be made, and what the final goal will be, in detail. There are a couple of reasons for this:

- You want to protect yourself legally. If you have problems with business operations because of the process, you will be able to show that it was used for a good reason. This will also demonstrate later on to any disgruntled parties that you behaved as a prudent business executive.
- If something goes wrong with the process, you'll know sooner rather than later. If the process causes some unexpected glitches with computer operations, proper documentation can show the team the most likely cause, or at least the nearest rat hole in which they can start looking. A well-presented, logical explanation of events is also good to have when dealing with angry stockholders. There's nothing like a spokesperson who hasn't a clue to incite the people with the pitchforks and torches. Despite extra effort spent on the paperwork, in the long run you'll find it will make the whole procedure go faster and easier. It's always cheaper to do something right the first time.

CONTROL CHANGE

Have you ever felt like your right hand didn't know what your left hand was doing? During the date update process, be prepared to feel that all the right hands don't know what the left hands are doing on the entire process team. Some programmers will be making changes to ready the programs to process the Year 2000 dates, while others will be continuing to meet the demands of day-to-day business.

Many computing organizations face this situation frequently due to program sharing, which we mentioned earlier. To deal with it, they put into place a process called *change control*. In different organizations, change control takes different forms; and it can be a manual process or an automated one. If your enterprise is dependent on a manual process, you will need to examine it for robustness: Can it handle the change process you will be implementing? If you have an automated software change management process in place, you may be ahead of the game. If you have automated software configuration management that manages shared component usage on a platform, you own the game. There are software change and configuration management systems available, but be aware that some are difficult to implement and may add an unnecessary burden to the date update project. They also add staff overhead to the normal operations of the computing organization and meet with a lot of resistance because they slow down the normal process of change.

Much of the impact of implementing change management is related to the preparedness of the organization. If you are well organized and familiar with the problem, implementing it is simple. If your organization clings to flexibility and individual initiative, you are pushing a large rock uphill. These products require meticulous inventorying of components and in-depth knowledge of the applications. Some are adaptive to organization structure; others require the organization to adapt to them. Determining which is right for you versus which is needed is an exercise for the strong at heart.

Creating a Test Environment

Creating a test environment is not an easy task. Computing people generally test on the same computer on which production programs are running, which essentially runs the testing of Year 2000 into a brick wall. As we have indicated, the problem is the system date. The dominant procedure for handling all processing is by determining what the current date is, which programmers do by reference to the computer clock. If you change the computer clock to sometime in the future, then the current production processing will be handled incorrectly.

There are several solutions to this problem, none of them ideal:

- Buy another computer so that one can run production and the other can run different dates. Problem: If you are testing different applications simultaneously, you need to have different computer dates for each one. The only answer: Buy several computers (possible only with generous budgets).

- Buy a software product that allows the programmers to artificially change the system date. Better, but we haven't seen one that accounts for all the nuances of a large computer shop, and a lot of study may be required to find the right one for your enterprise. In some cases, too, more than one will have to be purchased.

- Replace all accesses to the system date with calls to a table. This can be achieved under program control so that testing can be accomplished. In addition, it can be left in so that during production the date will continue to access the date supplied by you instead of the computer manufacturer. Downside: Who will be responsible for maintaining this calendar? That is the question that was answered by having the computer manufacturer supply the date. Besides the computer's system, software still uses that system date. What happens if the two dates get out of synchronization?

We warned you: no easy answers. But there is another alternative. Some disaster-recovery computer services are providing special testing environments. For a fee, you can transfer your testing processing to their computers. This means you won't have to buy additional machines.

One word of caution: Plan on spending more money on computer storage devices, because changing and testing at any level requires more space. You may recover some space by deleting programs that nobody uses, but you will need more. And don't forget, everybody else will need more storage devices, too. Production capacity may not be able to keep up with demand.

Selecting Tools

You need tools; no ifs, ands, or buts about it. Automation will help with all segments of the Year 2000 update process. Costs can be reduced by proper selection of tools and the right plan to implement them. Tools can improve productivity through better quality, speed, and completeness—when properly applied. Our experience indicates that the cost of the conversion can be reduced from 15 to 35 percent, depending on the tools used and the kinds of programming languages they have to work with. Unfortunately, no one single tool will do the job by itself.

Take a look at the following table. It is an example of the project automation we believe could be available, if all conditions are optimal, to a typical large computer shop.

Activity	Percent of Total Process	Percent of Task Automated or Assisted	Percent Saved of Total Process
Inventory (Location of Date Objects)	1%	80%	0.8%
Planning (Deciding what to change and when)	3%	27%	0.81%
Analysis (Specification of design changes)	14%	10%	1.4%
Update (Expansion of date fields, data and logic)	16%	20%	3.2%
Testing (Unit, Systems, and Integration Testing)	42%	40%	16.8%
Migration (Production transition, data change, and training)	5%	20%	1.0%
Management (Change, project, process, resource)	19%	33%	6.27%
		Total saved	30.28%

It is important to note that this example indicates this shop *could,* not necessarily *will,* achieve a 30 percent productivity improvement for the entire project. The caveat springs from the "if" statement preceding: "*if* properly applied." Most computer programmers and managers typically know how to use only about two-thirds of the tools they own, for very understandable reasons: Not all of these tools have been useful to them in the past. It takes time to learn how to use tools; knowledge of how to use tools is lost when the tools are not used on a regular basis; and knowledge becomes obsolete as the tools are updated by the vendor. Here are some interesting observations:

- It takes an average of three months for a person to be trained and become proficient in the use of a given tool.
- The average person can learn no more than two tools of different categories at one time and achieve competency in the same period.
- The Year 2000 update process may require as many as 30 or 40 different tools, depending on the operating system and the number of computers and computer languages.

Assuming no tools are currently available, an individual would not become proficient using all the update tools for three years. But consider these other observations to counterbalance the preceding:

- It is a rare organization that does not have some tools already.
- Some computers are sold with many tools that support the process.
- COBOL, the most prevalent computer language, is supported by many tools.
- Many tools work on PCs, meaning they are easier to use and make less of a demand on the main computer. (However, there is a steep learning curve if the staff is unfamiliar with PCs.)

◆ Optimal automation may achieve a 38 percent performance improvement with a total investment of less than 7 percent of the equivalent wage investment.

CODE CHANGE TOOLS

Code change tools can be used to alter computer code, create file conversion programs, and build database bridges. But it is essential to be aware before investing in these tools that, at best, they can be implemented to automate an activity that amounts to a maximum of 16 percent of the total project effort. Generally speaking, we have found they work best for straightforward changes and in support of the most common programming languages. Most work only with COBOL written for IBM mainframe—370 architecture or later—platforms. They are designed to work with expanding two-digit date fields to four-digit fields. Few attempt to make changes to the process instructions. Nearly all require the customer to define date "seeds" identifying date fields. Many lists of seeds miss a lot of dates because the staff does not recognize the dates, or the application cannot trace them through redefinition, levels of definitions, introduction of aliases, or levels of shared code modules. Some claim to insert logic to "window" the dates, interpreting the century as 19 or 20 based on parameters defined by you. This has already gotten many organizations into trouble because the window can change depending on the data. We have seen such window changes as many as five times within a single program. Automatic insertion of logical century assignment is the most dangerous practice we know. Tools of this type are being announced weekly, and everyone claims to have the "solution of the century."

Some vendors of these change tools will offer to take your code, date field "seeds" (rules for identifying date fields), and "window" requirements, make the changes, and give the modified code back to you, compiled or ready to compile (e.g., Matridigm). Others will bring these programs on-site (e.g., Data Dimensions' Ardes Engine) or sell the product for you to run (Prince Software's Translate 2000).

Unfortunately, our research into the viability of these tools has turned up disturbing findings relating to cost-effectiveness. Although these programs seem to complete date field expansions effectively, they cannot redesign processes. Thus, charges for such services have to be measured against the anticipated total of 16 percent of the total cost. This cost includes finding, off-loading, packaging, and so on that is done by the enterprise and not necessarily by the vendor. If your forecast says you should expect to pay 16 percent for code change, and the vendor cost is 50 percent, you will be overpaying for the product or service.

Whenever sending programs through a rule-based update process, you must know which rules they employ to change the code and how they make those changes; that way you can anticipate things they don't change and prepare for errors when they change things they shouldn't. In general, our advice is to use these code change tools, but don't expect too much and you will not be disappointed. The advantage is that these programs are good at imposing standards; but we've yet to find a tool of this sort that can provide an average accuracy of better than 85 percent (some applications that employ unusual constructs may achieve only half that accuracy), which means that a programmer must still go through all the code and identify sections that the automated process missed.

The reason these tools are limited in their effectiveness is that they can't anticipate the creativity of programmers. For example, on computers that don't have the space or the ability to process four-digit years, programmers have been forced to use several single-digit century options. A common solution is to store the century as a single-digit logic flag: A century indicator is set for 0 = 19 and 1 = 20. (Even IBM isn't consistent. In some equipment, 0 is used before the years 1940 through 1999, while 1 is used for the years 2000 through 2039.) Some enterprises use $0 = 1800$, $1 = 1900$, and $2 = 2000$. Another variation uses signed values, where 1900 has the value of 0; 1 or +1 represents 2000; and −1 represents 1800.

Systems programmers frequently use elapsed time. The first step is to choose a starting or base date. IBM talks about using Lilian dates, which start at October 15, 1582 (the date the Gregorian calendar was adopted). Dates of January 1, 1600, and January 3, 1980 are also often used as base dates. The date values stored are not true dates, but the number of days elapsed from the base date to the date intended. If the base date is January 3, 1980, and the date to be represented is March 1, 1980, the value stored is 58. Since the date itself is not stored, anytime the data is to be treated as a real date it must be converted by a program routine.

Other techniques that change dates for storage include displacement, modulo, and nines complement. The *displacement* technique subtracts the year from 2000 so that 1995 is stored as the value 5, while the value for 2005 is −5. The *modulo* technique uses a base year (e.g., 1964) and stores the difference so that for 1995, the value 31 is stored, and for 2005, 41 is stored. The *nines complement* technique subtracts the two-digit value of the year from 99 so that for 1995 the value stored is 04, and for 2005 it is 94. All these techniques require an arithmetic step in each place the date is validated, stored, retrieved, and displayed. Sorting can be tricky, too; using the nines complement, values for dates 1998 through 2002 are 01, 00, 99, 98, and 97.

An alternative programming method assigns century values by adding 30 to the year and comparing the two-digit result to 30. Any calculated value of less than 30 is assigned a century value of 19, and any value equal or greater is a century value of 20. For example, 1995 plus 30 results in 25, so the century is 19. Likewise, for the year 2000, the calculated value is 30 and the century is 20. Sorting is simplified by this method, but other complications arise. For a date prior to 1970, you will need to use a value greater than 30. When date ranges span a wide time frame within a set of dates, different incremental values are required within the same program.

Confused? We certainly are; and the preceding is just a small sample. We have found more than 40 different typical date formats in which to store dates. As you can imagine, finding a tool that handles all the common and the uncommon routines will be difficult if not impossible. The bottom line, then, when using these tools, is to know what they do and don't do, and you will achieve some effective help.

Choosing and Executing a Process Pilot

Time for the dress rehearsal. You have established standards, determined an update process, and selected tools that you can reasonably use on your computer programming date problem. It is time to decide where to start. It is imperative to perform a pilot process in order to identify problems and to establish a reliable time frame for the real thing—trust us, the first application through the process typically takes three times longer than you planned.

Plan your first project around some small system that you believe could be updated in a month. Make sure that it is *typical of the applications in the environment;* that is, uses the primary programming and operating platform (computer, operating system, programming languages, data management system, and communications process). Then do the following:

- Employ the tools that you already own and plan to use throughout.
- Enforce the standards.
- Rewrite any process step that doesn't work.
- Design alternative processes. (It may take more than one process to do a single activity due to languages, criticality of the component, the fact that it is shared, etc.)

When you are done, review your results against expectations. You are bound to find justification for automating some additional tasks.

The following are a few additional suggestions we have gleaned from the experience of others in regard to staffing the update process: Do not leave it up to the computer people who normally support the applications. They will try to fix things that are technologically imperfect. They will try to fold in changes that the computer users have been requesting for years. They will generally delegate the changes downward to the least experienced person on the team. In general, they will not be efficient.

After you complete your first pilot process and make the necessary corrections, do another pilot and measure the results, then use it to adjust the estimates in your budget.

Managing the Fix

The purpose of this chapter is twofold: (1) to consolidate and reiterate the lessons learned in the first four chapters; and (2) to prime you for the nuts and bolts of Chapters 5 through 10, which is where we tell you how to get the most from your staff, how to approach the workload, how to automate, what's in the toolbox, and where to get help when you need it.

They Who Hesitate Are Lost

Let's put you in motion. It's revealing to note that one of the most frequently accessed pages on the Year 2000 forum on the Internet is titled "Reasons for Doing Nothing." If you want to be amused, go there (www.year2000.com), but don't for a minute think that this problem isn't epidemic. Remember, it is human nature to laugh at those things that intimidate us the most.

Arthur C. Clarke, in his book *The Ghost from the Grand Banks* (Bantam Spectra, 1990), writes:

During the closing years of the century, most of the world's star-class programmers were engaged in the race to develop a "Vaccine '99"; it had become a kind of Holy Grail. Several faulty versions were issued as early as 1997—and wiped out any purchasers who hastened to test them before making adequate backups. The lawyers did very well out of the ensuing suits and countersuits.

Even if a Year 2000 "vaccine" is developed, the first versions are likely to have unwanted effects. More effective versions may come too late, or at too high a price. Remember, this silver bullet has to find all the dates, redesign data-handling processes, change the code, test the old date processes, test the new date processes, migrate code from old versions to new, make decisions about when and how to change things *without* tripping over decisions it makes about other applications, external data sharing, and spontaneous vendor solutions.

Probably the most knowledgeable organization in the world on computer statistics is Software Productivity Research, Inc., headed by Capers Jones. His estimates (published in the white paper "The Economic Impact of the Year 2000 Software Problem in the United States," www.spr.com, which is *must* reading) state that there are about 1.92 million professional software personnel in the United States, including managers, operations staff, and other nonprogrammers; and there are 32.4 million applications—*not counting* spreadsheets, which are produced primarily by noncomputing professionals. This means that each professional has to update something like 20 or more applications between now and the year 2000! Putting that in everyday terms, it means that your current staff will be more precious than gold.

It is time to begin—now. The days and weeks are ebbing away even as you read this. The sooner you begin this project, the better your chances of protecting your business from Year 2000 fallout.

Delay, and you put everything at risk. One very real risk, which we've only mentioned in passing thus far, is from litigation.

Capers Jones, in the aforementioned white paper, anticipates four classes of litigation:

- Litigation filed by clients whose finances or investments have been damaged.
- Litigation filed by shareholders of companies whose software does not safely make the Year 2000 transition.
- Litigation associated with any deaths or injuries derived from the Year 2000 problem.
- Class-action litigation filed by various affected customers of computers or software packages.

He adds, "For every dollar not spent on repairing the Year 2000 problem, the anticipated costs of litigation and potential damages will probably amount to more than $10." He notes that in the United States, where people are quick to take things into court, costs and damage awards could mount to 20 times larger than the actual cost of making the code changes. At the very least, he cautions that senior corporate executives who do not exercise "fiduciary responsibility to act in the best interests of the shareholders" will see their careers damaged, if not ended.

Many cases will go to trial before the Year 2000 because of systems failing due to dates such as 98 and 99 having special significance. These court cases will place an additional drain on management and on programming personnel as they are subjected to court appearances. Still other programmers may find new careers as expert witnesses.

Jones also validates our estimation that an enterprise starting in 1997 is likely to get through only about 80 percent of its applications; if it waits until 1999, only 30 percent. And even conceding that only 30 percent of the applications may be critical to the business of the enterprise, that 30 percent is probably attached by data to another 40 percent of the other applications that won't make the transition in time. At best, the organization will be crippled; at worst, it will no longer exist.

But don't forget: Risk and opportunity go hand in hand. There really are silver linings in these clouds. Here are a few of them:

- Consolidating these libraries and eliminating just-in-case data storage enables some companies to recover up to 40 percent of their program storage space. Eliminating dead files certainly can't hurt, and it may well help, because using four-digit years, along with other methods for assuring the computer knows what day it is, will take up more room; you will have more room once you clean closets.

- You will realize that not all reports have to go to all the people in your organization. In a documented instance, one department didn't realize for three months after being accidentally cut off that it wasn't getting its reports, and a couple of offices never noticed.

- You will have the opportunity to purchase or consolidate other enterprises as they are overwhelmed by the effort required to make changes and repair failing applications.

- Standardized date systems throughout the whole company will benefit staff, too, not just the computers. And, as a bonus, people may even develop a more professional attitude toward their own machines.

- Getting a handle on your software inventory will turn out to be just as important as tracking your inventory of supplies and work—and just as profitable, too. You'll eliminate marginal functions that serve little purpose.

- At the end of the process, you will know precisely which of your computer applications are important, and this will help you determine how to prioritize future investments.

- Working with your suppliers, vendors, and customers will go a long way toward reducing your own future data exchange problems. Ensuring they don't have Year 2000 problems will net long-term goodwill rewards, as all of you realize your mutual business dependency.

- Budgets that have been tight for years will be relaxed, which will allow some organizations to update software that hasn't been fixed since the first episode of the original *Star Trek* series. The same goes for hardware. Eliminating ancient hardware will mean eliminating personnel headaches—trying to train someone to work on those antiques.

- Just finding what's there may uncover hidden treasure. Many employees squirreled away programs and data that nobody else knows exists. Some enterprises have had to keep two versions of the same software for years and spend money on maintenance and version management. That savings can help pay for this work.

- Applying configuration management techniques to oversee your systems software, tools, and vendor application packages will cut down on labor costs (and frankly, after this conversion process, employees will just want to go home anyway).

Instant Replay

We've borrowed our Chapter 5 title from Michelle Callow of IBM, who used it as the title of her speech at the Central Computer and Telecommunications Agency Conference Forum in Norwich, England, in April 1996, where she mentioned the following factors as critical for success in solving the Year 2000 problem:

Management commitment
Definition and redefinition

Scheduling and resources

Monitoring and feedback

Communication

Exception handling

User consultation and acceptance

Determination to succeed

With these factors in mind, it is time to take the "ball to the hole," as they say in basketball. In this section we will recap the highlights from the first part of the book so the information will be fresh in your mind.

Although the Year 2000 problem is directly related to dates, it is an indirect outcome of the following:

- The human desire to save time and effort
- The legacy of the initial high cost of technology
- The legacy of data that was stored in the form that best met the first two reasons

The nature of the problem is manifest in its worst form in our computers, which will be unable to do the following:

- Date arithmetic correctly
- Compare dates correctly
- Sort dates in the proper sequence

The problem is not getting a lot of serious press for these reasons:

- It's perceived as something too big to be real.
- There are serious implications to the survival of government and financial infrastructures.
- Most large organizations take a long time to get enough data to describe their problem. CIBC, a large, well-managed Canadian

bank, experienced 15 months elapsed time to inventory their applications, estimate and analyze what they have, and determine what they want to do about fixing them. They are not the only ones. We have seen other organizations spend a year looking at tools and conducting pilots with no appreciable movement toward getting the change process started.

- Many organizations are still trying to figure out what to do about the problem; nobody wants to appear incapable of dealing with it.

The fact is, the following large sectors of the economy are already working on the problem:

Governments at all levels
Financial institutions
Public utilities
Transportation providers

The Year 2000 problem is not limited to legacy programs, mainframe computers, or specific programming languages, but also affects the following:

- Embedded systems—computers built into machinery
- Obsolete computers
- Obsolete languages and programs
- Business processes that employ dates
- Vendors that won't or can't fix their products in time
- Suppliers that can't fix their problems
- Customers who will not understand

To repair the problem will require the following:

- Finding the software
- Identifying and fixing existing, but unrealized, date problems

- Converting old versions of software to new versions that are supported
- Replacing and expanding hardware
- Purchasing computer resources and software tools
- Recovering lost computer code
- Retraining staff
- Redesigning the software

Related and possibly concomitant problems include the following:

- Failure to solve the problem may result in litigation drawing away money and staff resources, possibly the loss of executives.
- Operations may be suspended by failures of internal systems.
- Operations may be interrupted by failures of infrastructure systems—heat, power, communications, transportation.
- Coordinating with vendors, suppliers, and customers will involve all management staff.

Costs of the repair will be both controllable and uncontrollable:

- *Controllable*

  - Internal software fixes and replacement
  - Internal hardware fixes and replacement
  - Business process changes

- *Uncontrollable*

  - Vendor delays, failures, and noncompliance to standards
  - Litigation costs
  - Staffing turnover and cost escalation
  - Failures of suppliers
  - Overlooked problems

The problem resolution is dependent on the following factors:

- Time
- Managing the large numbers
- Management decision making
- An unmovable deadline

Two parallel processes must take place in order to get the problem under control: planning and preparation. *Planning* includes the following component activities:

- Locating software and hardware components
- Testing date processes
- Estimating the repair/replacement costs
- Surveying vendors and scheduling changes
- Performing triage on the applications
- Sequencing the work effort
- Building awareness
- Obtaining resources and forming a team

Preparation includes the following component activities:

- Setting standards
- Creating an update process
- Creating a controlled change environment
- Establishing a testing environment
- Selecting tools
- Choosing and executing a process pilot

The following vehicles will tend to drive the project to failure:

- Doing nothing or getting bogged down in decision making
- Waiting for somebody or some company to develop a silver bullet

- Adding too many other jobs to fixing this problem
- Expecting everything to happen on a schedule
- Expecting to keep all people on board for the entire project
- Trying to accomplish everything all at once
- Working without a plan

The imperatives propelling you to address this problem are (1) staying in business and (2) minimizing litigation costs. The long-term rewards are as follows:

- Cleaning the closet
- Eliminating unnecessary reports and functions
- Getting the leverage to buy out competitors
- Standardizing; improving quality
- Eliminating marginally profitable products
- Building closer relationships with suppliers, vendors, customers
- Finding resources that can save time and money in the future
- Establishing controls over the computing environment

There is a Year 2000 problem. Most business computers and applications are at risk; your computers and applications are at risk. Ask yourself: How long can my company last without them? If you understand all the suggestions and recommendations we have presented, you are ready to tackle the Year 2000 problem at your organization or enterprise.

Chapter Six

Power to the People

The single most critical resource you have available for fixing the Year 2000 problem in your organization is your trained and experienced staff. Twenty percent of the work involves management: resource (people, hardware, tools) management, change management, configuration management, and process management. Even work performed by nonmanagement personnel will require supervision. This includes inventorying and planning (4 percent), analyzing the code to be changed and deciding how to change it (14 percent), changing the code and building data-handling programs (16 percent), testing the changed and developed programs (42 percent), and finally, changing the data and putting the programs into production use (5 percent).

Manual Labor

Considering we are talking about implementing changes to computerized systems, it may surprise you to learn that most of the work on the Year 2000 update project is manual. Let's start with how the roles of the managers break out:

- *Change management* requires a person knowledgeable of priorities and schedules to determine what is to be changed and when.
- *Configuration management* uses tools or keeps track of components to coordinate changes to each of the involved sectors to ensure that all parts reach production at the same time, minimizing "code freeze" duration.
- *Process management* identifies process difficulties, opportunities for improvements, and work processes that can be handled by less-skilled staff. They also manage personnel turnover that requires recruiting and retraining, which imposes a heavy burden on the resources you need most—your most knowledgeable staff.
- *Resource management* involves making sure the people and hardware resources are available to make the changes. It requires constant attention to ascertain that decision makers are available to solve problems and determine which design changes will be implemented. It also involves verifying that training happens when and for whom it is needed.

Even after you have minimized decision making by imposing standards and simplifying the process, you will find another 7 to 10 percent of the update effort involves analysis, because although the scanning performed in the estimating process will locate many dates, it will not find them all—meaning they will have to be isolated at analysis time. Remember, every date is suspect, even those that appear to include four-digit designations. Why? Because there are applications in which a century field has been allocated but never used, or one in which four digits have been moved into the two-digit-year field where the century has been lost in the truncation process. In other situations, a literal 19 has been inserted into the century position of every year. Finally, even processes that involve only day calculations may be in error, because routines that determine the day of the week might be using a calendar that rolls to the year 1900, resulting in every day of the week appearing incorrectly.

Although using tools to implement code changes will be helpful, you will find that staffing demands will be high for redesigning the code. And, if you have purchased tools that employ rule-based processing, you will have to spend staff time identifying rule requirements and testing those rules. Or, if you can create your own rules, you will find time requirements to be just as high as making the code changes. Each rule has to be programmed and tested. The more rules that are created, the more difficult it becomes to create a rule that does not conflict with another. The testing has to find every situation where the rule could be applied and then make sure that it works and the code is changed in the intended way. If you are dependent on a vendor to provide those rules, you will still have to manage that process.

TIME IN A BOTTLE

During the Year 2000 update process, most of your staff time will be allocated to testing. The typical programming staff will discover that creating test scripts, preparing test data, executing, and validating tests will absorb 40 percent of the total project effort. Some strategies (which we will explain later) can reduce that effort in some situations, but in general, testing is a time-consuming part of the process. Further, keeping track of test data and comparison files will add another burden to your staff if they are unfamiliar with regression testing. You will find regression testing is essential because you will need to retest some programs over and over because of linkages to many other applications that can't all be changed at the same time.

HEADING SOUTH

Migration, the process of changing data and file definitions, retraining application users, and moving applications into production, will be significantly complicated in the update process. The typical data processing organization performs one or two migrations a month, and usually schedules them for a weekend to minimize impact on the workload and to provide a buffer against glitches. In large organizations, the migration effort may require that multiple applications be moved from testing to production in a single weekend; some migrations may have to be performed during the workweek.

A Project by Any Other Name

We have used the term *project manager* to describe the leader of the Year 2000 update effort. It is probably a misnomer, because a project is loosely defined as achievement of a goal by completing a number of predetermined tasks. But with the Year 2000 problem, technically we do not have a project, we have a program, because all we have is a *plan* to execute a number of projects. This may appear to be an inconsequential distinction, but it is not. Programs are managed differently from projects. A project is achieved by committing the appropriate resources to a predefined set of tasks. The management of a project thus involves getting the right resources assigned to the task, then making sure it is completed as required. The focus is on what you do, not how you do it.

Program management takes into account that you don't have control over all the resources. It focuses on *how* you work to make sure that you achieve the best you can with the resources you do have. Thus program managers have significantly more latitude for decision making. Project managers can create a plan, present it to management, and negotiate schedules, resources, and authority because all the requirements are known, whereas a program manager lays on the table intentions—an estimate of the sequence of actions that will be taken, a requirement for cooperation. The program manager is given far more power to act than the project manager.

Many organizations already employ one or more project managers. The individuals in these roles often have too little authority and too narrow a scope within the organization to effectively carry out the job of the program manager that will be required on the Year 2000 effort. We recommend that those organizations institute a new title to distinguish the authority invested in the leader of the effort, although we will continue to use the term *project manager* here for consistency.

Centralized Authority

Many enterprises have decentralized data processing organizations so that responsibility for data processing is divided along functional lines. While this gives the functional organizations more control over data processing priorities and more direct accountability for the budgets, it has created an environment of parochialism. For example, many applications are duplicated. You may find your organization burdened with a dozen General Ledger Systems and several Payroll Systems. During the Year 2000 triage process—determining where to assign increasingly scarce resources first—the cost of this duplication becomes apparent. Because of the desire to retain control and minimize the impact on each organization, they will fight to retain their versions, thereby delaying the start of the work.

At this juncture, you may have to make some tough decisions. Should you:

- Recentralize some applications?
- Impose one application solution on all the organizations?
- Undertake simultaneous changes to all the applications at the same time?
- Coordinate the passing of data in different formats?

These decisions cannot be made by a project manager with a reporting relationship to a single line authority. They must be made by an individual who puts the interests of the enterprise ahead of departmental concerns. This person must be able to do this in an environment divorced from politics; otherwise the decisions may come too late to prevent widespread problems. The project manager must have the authority to make these decisions with limited accountability, a capability usually found only at the upper layers of the enterprise.

Even those enterprises that have retained strong centralized data processing organizations discover that some decisions take too long to make. These enterprises have delegated the budgets for data processing to the functional operations groups, usually in organizations where managers compete on the basis of budget management. In such organizations the cost of the repair may invoke a heavy penalty on an individual manager. The repair bill will be highest in accounting and human resource organizations where date-dependent processing is widespread. Other organizations may have smaller price tags; for example, engineering and manufacturing systems generally have fewer date-dependent processes. In such enterprises, the politics of funding the project often cause delays in initiating fixes.

Internal politics also impose delays to the project, which subsequently increases costs. Where applications are shared by more than one organization, funding must be obtained from each of the organizations in order to perform the work, and usually it is difficult to obtain such approvals. Priorities within one or more of those organizations will delay allocation of people or financial resources.

True, workarounds to delays can be implemented, but this, too, may add to the expense. For example, some portions of an application may have event horizons that are earlier for one part of the application than for others, thus forcing you to build additional data interfaces that later have to be removed. This piece of the application may affect one part of the enterprise that has only a minor interest in the whole application, and the primary application owner may not want to fund the work. Again, only a strong centralized authority can cut through the red tape to avoid additional costs and focus the resources in the best interests of the enterprise.

ORGANIZE FOR SUCCESS

We have already talked about the need to assign a central program manager/leader. It is time now to talk about the other key players who will work for and with that leader. The number of people required will vary by organization size and the talents of the individuals involved; nevertheless, we believe that each of the following roles should be accounted for in one form or another.

Awareness Coordinator

The awareness coordinator performs different functions during the project. At the outset, this person performs the role of publicist, defining and explaining the problem, which will be a full-time job. One difficulty for the person filling this role is that outside the data processing organization there will no doubt be significant resistance to the cost of doing work that has no apparent payoff. Later, this job will change to one of coordination.

The awareness coordinator will prepare the application support teams to release their applications for changes to the date processes, while keeping them consistent with business changes. The person in this role also must ensure that the applications can continue to run while operating system software is changed and vendor software changes are implemented.

The awareness coordinator also works with end users. A good coordinator will uncover context problems that occur when users do things such as putting 00 or 99 in the year fields to force sorting of records in a way that simplifies the use of the data. The coordinator may also find places where users have discovered weaknesses in the system, such as a failure to adequately validate data entry resulting in nonnumeric data appearing in date fields. Discovery prevents two problems: (1) the failure of the system when it is put back into production (testers check only for what they expect, not for what they don't know) and (2) the wrath of users who find they have no way to perform a function they have been performing for years.

The awareness coordinator may also double as end-user trainer. When it is necessary for the data processing staff to change the way an application accepts or presents data, the awareness coordinator will be in the best position to explain the necessity and the reason for the solution being implemented.

Vendor Manager

No one person will be more important than the one who keeps track of all the vendors. As you now realize, changes will be made in hardware, application and system software, and incoming and outgoing data. The latter—data changes—may include requirements imposed by regulatory agencies, suppliers, or clients.

Because software vendors will not be eager to make commitment dates, the vendor manager will have to stay on top of the vendors to track changes in schedules and the way they are addressing the date problem within their products. While standards do exist, survival is the issue for many of these companies, and they will be doing what they can for the least expense. As we warned early in the book, do not be surprised if some of these vendors simply give up and go out of business. And even if you have copies of the vendor's code in escrow in a safe-deposit box somewhere, it will probably not prove to be of much use. Undocumented code of any type poses a daunting task for any organization. The vendor manager will have to try to anticipate late or failed deliveries.

Supplier-Chain Manager

We cannot even imagine an enterprise that is not dependent on outside providers. Consequently, utilities, service providers, and commodity vendors will all need to be tracked. Many will be affected by changes to the organization's applications, which may be as minimal as report or form changes, or as significant as the requirements for data in formats needed for millennium-compliant applications. The supplier-chain manager may have to work with other organizations to coordinate these demands on suppliers.

The supplier-chain manager also fills the role of information provider to the supplier, monitoring them to make sure they take the date problem seriously and to assess the supplier's response. If the supplier is not going to meet your deadline, it is the supplier-chain manager's responsibility to determine what action to take: to delay schedules, acquire additional reserves, or find a new supplier.

Technical Coordinator

The technical coordinator manages changes to the data processing environment. As changes are made to the systems software, this person will work to minimize the testing and coordinate changes to the applications. This person will also work with the hardware and systems software providers to determine the impact of vendor decisions on the organization's data processing capability and to coordinate hardware replacement and migrations with the vendors and the staff.

The technical coordinator may also be required to direct replacement of the PCs that cannot be upgraded to function properly beyond December 31, 1999. After the century change, many applications will not be able to run under the current operating system; for example, those using DOS versions that are no longer supported. Many vendors will move to the latest version of MS Windows, which may require more memory or even processor speed changes that will force the organization to replace its hardware. And older PCs that have been put into use as printer servers or in other roles may not be able to perform those menial functions any longer because their internal clocks will not function as required to show the correct date.

Quality Assurance Manager

This role does not exist in most organizations today. It was abandoned when it became popular to make everyone in the data processing organization accountable for quality. But in this project, the quality assurance manager will play a key role in containing the problem by monitoring the acquisition of software to ensure that it's all 2000-compliant and by monitoring routines to ascertain they handle dates according to standards.

Testing is also the responsibility of the quality assurance manager. He or she must ensure that testing goes beyond proving that the application works the way it is supposed to. He or she must "guarantee" that the applications cannot be "broken." This means, for example, in the case of the century change, testing not only for 1999 but for 2099 as well. If dates are stored in binary formats, the quality assurance manager will have to test all binary combinations to make sure that they are converted correctly. Finally, he or she will have to enforce testing of data coming in from the outside to make sure that internal data is not corrupted.

Purchasing Coordinator

The purchasing coordinator is the liaison with the purchasing department, the one who influences vendors to meet commitments. This person also works with purchasing to assure that new purchases are century-compliant.

Legal Coordinator

One or more people from the enterprise's legal staff may be required on the team. A legal presence is necessary not only to work with purchase and maintenance contracts, but also to make sure that contracts entered into by the enterprise include force majeure clauses, which make nonperformance due to others' inability to overcome Year 2000 problems as excusable as any other natural disaster.

Legal staff members play a key role in defining product compliance, risks, and negotiating prices reflective of millennium compliance benefits and risks. They will work with vendors who have changed product names to make sure that the vendor retains responsibility under the terms of any contracts. If you need to make changes to vendor software, they will obtain the appropriate releases. They will renegotiate services for products whose contracts have lapsed or that have had warranties voided due to unauthorized code changes.

The legal coordinator will work with accountants, executive management, and the board of directors to minimize financial liabilities, continuing coverage by director and officer insurance, and business continuation insurance. The legal coordinator will also play a key role in keeping the enterprise out of collateral litigation due to failure to meet regulations, injury or death arising out of supplier failures, or actions based on incorrect data.

Process Manager

Throughout the correction process, it is important to oversee the update team, because measurement of daily work may be key to the success of the project overall. To repeat the opening of this chapter: People are your most important resource; you cannot afford to have anyone sitting on his or her hands waiting for others. The process manager will be responsible for finding these problems and identifying the causes and possible solutions.

From time to time the process manager also will define tool requirements and process changes, or make recommendations for further training or staff alterations. This will require the process manager to constantly search for new tools. He or she may participate in testing and evaluation of tools to see how they perform. The process manager also needs to keep abreast of how well tool vendors are responding to problem reports and difficulties found with the tools owned.

Tools Manager

Software tools will not remain static; they will change as vendors receive additional requirements and make alterations to add functions or fix what does not always work. The tools manager will coordinate these changes, provide instruction, communicate requirements, and make sure that new people receive coaching on the use of the tools.

The tools manager will also supervise the internal development of tools to handle unique processes that are not supported by vendor-supplied tools. Internally developed tools may change data, track suppliers, handle special file accesses, alter enterprise calendars, or provide date processes that are unique to the enterprise.

The Others

Obviously, it will be necessary to have on staff those people—analysts and programmers—who actually make the changes to the enterprise's software. But this is not as simple as just assigning everyone to a change team. There will be special demands. You will still have to support applications that have not been made century-compliant as regulatory and data requirement changes are made by other organizations. Some staff may have to write new technical file interface programs, or take on PC rescue missions to save end-user-created programs that require changes, but for which the end user lacks resources to implement those changes. This may require learning PC database applications and spreadsheet macrolanguages.

Process Management and Continuous Improvement

Those enterprises that are careful to define the process, measure the workflow through each stage, and then take action to improve that workflow will achieve the best results in managing both costs and cycle time. They also will be best able to adapt to changes in schedules, shifting priorities, and defections in the workforce.

Setting up a process management environment is a three-step activity:

1. Defining the activity
2. Describing the work
3. Measuring the work

DEFINING THE ACTIVITY

Activity definition involves identification of all activities required by the organization to update the system, from preparation to change applications through migration to production. Defining the activity can be done by bringing the representatives of the various line organizations together in a design session, which may take from one to three days depending on the complexity of the environment. We suggest it be done on the basis of the computing platform because the process differs for each. The first effort will take longer, because the processes that follow need only to identify differences, and this can often be completed in hours rather than days.

During this step, you identify accountability for each activity. It is also necessary so that activities are delineated. Many people prefer to do this by separating activities into sets of tasks that are related but that report to different people. This method tends to resist change and improvement, however; only by "breaking the activity" at the lines of authority is it possible for a change to be made, which means the process ends when accountability for the product is transferred to another person. While a contractor may be responsible for building the whole house, he or she makes the plumber accountable for the plumbing, the electrician accountable for wiring, and so on. In IT organizations, different people have specific domains for which they are responsible. Nobody is allowed to cross those lines of authority.

Other activity delimiters include changes in skill requirements and the use of specific hardware or software tools. For example, the knowledge requirements for making changes to a COBOL program are significantly different from those required to make changes to an assembler language program. They use different talents, may employ different tools, and require variable time frames to obtain the same effective throughput. If, for example, the activity is moved from one computer to another, the person will require a different set of skills (e.g., operating the computer) and knowledge (e.g., working with operating systems, job scheduling languages, and compilers). This will be important if the activity is to be improved later.

DESCRIBING THE WORK

Workflow description is done by the people who do the work. Taking the process definition prepared in the first step, they perform a test update project. We recommend a small project consisting of not more than 100,000 lines of code. The system selected should be one that will exercise as many of the defined activities as possible. For instance, in an environment that uses database management, communications management, and PC development tools, you will want to select an application in which all of these are encountered and therefore can be subjected to the update procedure.

Throughout the process, the workflow definition team should document each task, the tools they use, and their knowledge requirements. When problems are encountered, the team should identify them and refer them to the person named accountable for those process activities. During this small test run, you may find that additional process activities are defined. At the end of the test, you should have a set of processes in which the inputs and outputs are clearly defined and the boundaries of responsibility are set.

MEASURING THE WORK

Measurement is key to achieving efficiency. However, do not expect to measure the test process, since that should be regarded as an exercise of documentation and problem resolution. A second test similar to the first will be necessary to determine process timing. Choose another small application similar in attributes to the first (but do not repeat the same application conversion, as familiarity will alter the effort measurements).

During the second test, ask someone *not involved* in the effort to define the volume and time attributes of the process. Establish anticipated time frames based on the skills of the people involved in performing the tasks so that allowances can be made for those with greater or lesser skill. At the end of this second run-through, you should be able to identify where the bottlenecks are caused by the inability to handle volume and dependencies on resources.

Following this second test, you should have enough information not only to manage the process, but to take a number of actions to improve workflow. You may decide to purchase or build a tool. You may choose to scale the work, creating more "pipeline" segments to distribute the work to several individuals. You may see the need to provide training in the use of tools, or to subdivide the activities.

REDUCING SKILL DEPENDENCIES

A well-documented process includes the three steps just defined and identifies how to deal with exceptions. At this juncture, decision making should be minimized, and the number of people included in communications should be reduced to a single person—the individual identified as accountable for a particular activity.

As the demands for skilled computer people increase, you will be faced with rising costs and, perhaps, increased defections from your current labor pool. The labor pool of experienced programmers with the knowledge required is finite. It can take a year, for example, to train a person in COBOL, DB2, and CICS, putting a drain on your staff while you train them. The demand for these people will rise and push salaries upward. Since most organizations have rules that limit the size of raises, you may fall behind the competition, thereby forcing your own people to go elsewhere. But these defections will be mitigated by having the processes clearly defined. A new person with the appropriate skills can be handed the descriptions of the processes they are expected to perform and become proficient in the shortest amount of time.

Once the process descriptions are completely defined, you can also begin distributing work to individuals who may not be fully skilled in all aspects of the work, or even familiar with the makeup of the organization. Many tedious and redundant tasks now performed by skilled computer experts can be performed by clerical staff already employed by the company. Many of these less demanding tasks are now being done by your most highly paid technical staff. The lack of process descriptions, low volume, and infrequency of the work required have prevented this from happening. You cannot bring a person into an organization and make him or her a part of the process in less than two days. If the work lasts only a day or two, bringing someone in is not practical. The advantage of solving this Year 2000 problem is that it creates new opportunities as the need to do many of these tasks becomes constant.

Less-skilled workers can be part of an assembly line: finding lines with dates in them, creating test data, changing screens or reports, and more. Key employees may be able to supervise the work of more staff because they won't be as involved in providing orientation, training, or coaching.

BUILDING A FACTORY

Many organizations have found it productive to build a "factory" to which the code is sent. This factory takes the existing code, makes the changes, compiles the code to make sure that it is error-free, and returns the code. These "factory workers" must be familiar with all the available date routines, know the tools to identify all the dates, and be able to use code update and editing tools to make the changes. They also should be able to identify processes that need redesign.

If standards have been established, factory personnel can use them as a guide to implement the changes. Where the standards fail to address the redesign work, they should create exception reports and return them to those who best understand the application and can make the necessary decisions or changes.

Normally, a factory includes a team that works with the application support staff. This team identifies and gathers the components to be changed and creates requirements for bridge programs and data conversion programs that can be built in the factory. They also define special testing requirements that will have to be performed after the code is processed by the factory.

At the back end of the factory, where the code has been changed but not tested, the same team that supports the preparation also facilitates processing the exceptions and scheduling tests. These staff members may be skilled at data creation using tools and may manage regression testing for the organization. Normally, the testing, data conversion, and migration are left to the application support teams.

Create Talent Pools

You will want to assess your staffing and perform a skills inventory. It is essential to identify critical talent requirements, which may fall into two distinct groups. The first is technical talent, those people who know the operating system software, the coding languages, and the available productivity and management tools. The second group includes those staff members who know the processes used by the enterprise, the applications, and their users.

The technical talent forms the skill backbone of the staff who change the code and move the code and data into production. This group should consist of programmers fluent in each of the languages employed; database administrators who know the data and file management tools employed; communications specialists who have knowledge of the communications management software; a technical support staff member familiar with the operating system as it was installed and all utilities that are provided to support it.

The second group provides your decision support and usually consists of experienced analysts and management personnel. Few people know more about the organization than the managers. They may be, or may have been, project managers, senior systems analysts, or even business analysts. They generally have come up through the ranks and been involved in the implementation of the systems. For the most part, these people should be familiar with the systems that have been identified as critical to the enterprise during the triage process.

Identifying these two groups has several benefits that will manifest themselves in the following discussions. The primary point here is that these people form the core update team, and thus will be critical to the success or failure of the entire project. These are the people who must be kept on staff at all costs. It is not, however, necessary that these individuals report to the project manager; rather, it is important that they be available to the project manager whenever required to provide training and advice to the teams performing changes.

"TIGER TEAMS"

Note that we did not say that anyone in the preceding two groups of critical talent should actually be involved in the changing of application code. Together, they "own" the context, or the environment, in which the decisions and changes are to be made. Consequently, you still need people experienced with date changes and problems.

Over the last five years we have found that knowledge of date processing and the way that dates are handled is more important than application knowledge. People familiar with date processing are better at making redesign decisions; they are less concerned about the application and thus less likely to make ancillary changes to improve performance or alter style. They also are more likely to enforce standards, use common date routines, identify processes that require business decisions, and employ tools. We call these people "tiger teams."

A tiger team often provides a significant productivity improvement factor. Working closely together to achieve a common goal, they are the most likely to continuously improve the process, to assimilate new tools, and to take pride in the speed and accuracy of their work. They generally are more willing to seek advice and expertise from the technical and organization specialists. Tiger teams also are more likely to create mechanisms to deal with conflict and thus handle it most diplomatically.

Forming Tiger Teams

We recommend that instead of delegating the correction problem to the organization as a whole, you form one or more tiger teams to perform the date changes. Select people who make good use of tools to perform their work. You may start the team with some of the critical talent pool members, but they should be replaced as soon as possible. Those people will be in constant demand to fill knowledge gaps and maintain progress toward deadlines. Tiger team members should be among those who most willingly accept change: They get involved with the newest computer languages, take advantage of technologies such as the Internet, and aggressively seek recognition.

The formation of tiger teams also solves a major problem that most organizations face. Sometimes, being assigned to the problem-repair team may be viewed as a demotion—after all, you are trying to keep your old systems alive, which means fixing old code (in other words, *maintenance*). Maintenance is often considered a task for the inexperienced. Many organizations that have tried to recruit internally for staff to fix old code have met with dismal failure. Nobody wants the job.

Creating tiger teams alters this picture. Everybody in an organization knows who the stars are. Getting these stars on a single team immediately gives the group a certain cachet. Membership on the team is then regarded as a learning experience and an opportunity. Should you lose a member of the team, it becomes easier to recruit replacements. As the members of the tiger teams become proficient with all the tools used in the process, they can be redeployed into the organization to serve as tool advocates and to provide guidance to teams involved in repairing applications that break down due to date problems.

"FLYING SQUAD"

And let's face it, things are going to break down. Between 1998 through 2000, we anticipate many system failures. Remember, you will not be able to test for everything, and these untested systems will create problems. To cope with them, we recommend the formation of a "flying squad." This squad should consist of from three to five of those critical talent pool members who are also skilled in making date changes and using all the tools at the enterprise's disposal. Whenever a breakdown occurs, the flying squad sends in a member to diagnose the problem and provide direction to the application support team to make the repairs. If the support team is inadequately skilled to make the changes in the time required, the flying-squad member can enlist the aid of their other team members to make the change and get the application back into production.

Flying-squad teammates can be gleaned from the tiger teams. They should be the most capable and most technically well rounded, because they will be faced with multiple platforms, languages, and crisis situations. This squad needs to be empowered to act. In many situations, members will need security clearance to access and make changes to the code or the data. A small group of trusted individuals can be given this level of authority and access.

Large organizations with multiple code development sites may find it efficient to create a flying squad at the beginning of the update project. This team can take the knowledge of how to define and establish an update process to each of the sites and build a process tailored to that site. A flying squad of this type could consist of no more than three people, each adept at process definition and facilitation, to focus on the topics of applications, quality assurance, and tools usage.

Incentives to Win

A discussion of getting the most from your staff would not be complete without addressing how to retain them. Earlier, we recommended that you identify your key staff members and determine how to ensure that they are satisfied with their positions in the update project. This requires that you consider the following factors.

Money is always an issue, of course. People experienced in executing and managing the date change process will be in great demand. But if you just raise the salaries of these people to meet the market demand, you will be faced with having a segment of your staff that makes more than the rest, causing dissatisfaction and promoting defection. At the same time, you will not be able to justify such high wages when the crisis is past, and you will be forced to let these people go. You could ask if they are subsequently willing to take reductions in pay, but even if they do, you will have to cope with a group of disgruntled people who know more about your enterprise's applications than anyone else—not an environment conducive to future success.

Therefore, we suggest that you institute an incentive program such as those often used by organizations involved in mergers. These incentives include retention bonuses: pay for remaining on the job through the crisis. In the case of the update project, the salaries of the key staff remain the same, but a fund is set up and continuously added to. As time passes, the fund grows larger. The amount paid into the fund can be adjusted to offset the market price for these people. The staff remaining through Year 2000 can share in the fund distribution. How much they get from the fund depends on how many people stay, how much is put into the fund, and the mechanism defined for distributing it (percent of salary, per person, job class, or merit are all options).

Companies that expect to do well by achieving early compliance may choose to set up a financial award program that includes stock incentives. Other enterprises may offer retirement packages to people who remain through the crisis. A combination of programs may be the best option to keep both younger and more senior staff.

Awarding vacation time is yet another option, especially for newer employees who would not otherwise be eligible. Providing for sabbaticals at the end of the crisis also is a significant enticement for experienced personnel. These sabbaticals can range from an extended time away to paid programs to learn new skills.

Many organizations have let their educational reimbursement programs languish. They have not kept pace with rising tuition rates, nor have they remained flexible so that employees can elect programs not directly involved with their work assignments. Thus, providing credits toward education to be obtained after work hours or after the crisis can be a powerful incentive to many. It will especially appeal to those who would like career changes and increased responsibility. Such programs benefit the enterprise, not only during the crisis but also later, when these people choose to remain with the enterprise as a result of the education benefits.

Empowerment can't be taken to the bank; nevertheless, it is a strong motivator. Building the workflow process creates significant opportunities for empowering the organization to improve itself. Reward systems that support empowerment—such as suggestion plans and acknowledgment awards—provide a motivation to stay with the enterprise, with the promise of future advancement and increased responsibility.

Chapter Seven

A Date with Destiny

I t's restating the obvious by now to say that the Year 2000 problem is caused by how dates are stored in computers; specifically, there's no standard way that we store these dates. This chapter delves deeper into the standardization factor and offers two approaches for confronting the date challenge destined to disrupt all our lives.

To begin, let's review some of the common ways dates are stored before we launch into the approaches for dealing with this convoluted situation:

- Dates can be stored as number strings, character strings, or a combination of the two.
- They can be four positions long (month and year), five positions (year and days), six positions (year, month, day in three different sequences), or more (the winner, so far, is 64 positions in length).
- They can be stored with a century prefix, with a century "flag," or without a century prefix.
- They can be stored with delimiters (for example, /, −, a blank space, or a period).

- They can be stored in strings, as a compressed numeric (where two digits exist in the same space as a character), or as a binary number.
- They can be stored with or without an arithmetic sign: $+/-$.

Conversely, some programmers don't store the date at all, but instead use a counter that calculates the number of clock cycles since some base date such as January 1, 1600, or January 4, 1980. Many of these clocks, because of the space allocated to the counter, will roll over to a value of zero during the next century.

Date	Complete Representation		Truncated Representation	
	Basic Format	**Ext. Format**	**Basic Format**	**Ext. Format**
April 15, 1995	19950415	1995-04-15	950415	95-04-15
April 15 (any yr.)	N/A	N/A	—0415	—04-15
15th of (any mo., yr.)	N/A	N/A	—15	N/A
April 1995	1995-04	N/A	-9504	-95-04
1995	1995	N/A	-95	N/A
1995 week 15, Sat.	1995W156	1995-W15-6	95W156	95-W15-6
1995 week 15	1995W15	1995-W15	95W15	95-W15
Any Saturday	N/A	N/A	–6	N/A
1995 day 105	1995105	1995-105	95105	95-105
×5 day 105 (any decade)	N/A	N/A	5-105	N/A
Day 105 of any year	N/A	N/A	-105	N/A

And the International Standards Organization (ISO) standard allows dates to be stored in all these ways:

(N/A = Not allowed)

Then there's the American National Standards Institute (ANSI), which says dates can:

1. Be represented as all numeric.
2. Be presented in year, month, day order.
3. Contain no delimiters.
4. Show months in the form 01 to 12.
5. Show days in Gregorian date views in the form 01 to 28, 29, 30, or 31 (based on month and accounting for leap years).

And to complicate things further, ANSI allows this alternative: The two high-order digits can be omitted if the century referenced is the current century. Of course, ANSI does require that when this representation is used, the phrase "Year of the Century" be employed in defining the representation. Another option is to use only one digit for the year. In such instances, you must use the term "Year of the Decade" in the description.

In the United States, programmers are subjected to the following standards, which cover representation of dates in ordinal, or Julian, formats as well as the representation of time. At a Year 2000 forum in 1996, a GTE representative shared the following list of the standards they are concerned with.

Domain	Standard
Department of Defense procurements	FIPS-4-1 (Revised 1996-03-25)
SQL	ANSI X3.135-1992, ISO-IEC 9075:1992, or FIPS 127-2
Exchange of call-billing data	Bellcore SR-STS-00320 (EMI)
Credit, debit and ATM cards	ISO-IEC 7813, or ISO 4909
Electronic commerce	ASC X12 (EDI draft std.), ISO 9735, or UN/EDIFACT
International concerns for interoperability	ISO 8601

But it would be naive, even foolhardy, to assume that everyone—or even anyone—has maintained these standards, ambiguous as they are. We have found instances that would defy rational explanation. Here's a sample:

- CYYMMDD—where C represents the two digits of the century; 0 is 19, 1 is 20 (there are some instances where 1 is equivalent to 18)
- SCYYMMDD—where S stands for a sign and −1 is 18, 0 is 19, and +1 is 20
- AAMMDD—where AA is an alphabetic with A0 equal to the year 2000, A1 the year 2001, B0 the year 2010
- SSSYY—where SSS represents the season

How to Approach Ground Double-Zero

All of this "standardization" has resulted in two common approaches to solving the Year 2000 date problem, but they require you to first ignore all the unusual date storage practices and focus on the most frequently used—the Gregorian YYMMDD, MMDDYY, and DDMMYY or the Ordinal/Julian YYDDD. The first approach is called the *logical approach;* the other is the *physical approach.* It would follow, then, that in most applications, it must be a simple matter of choosing the approach that is right for you and your enterprise. But in keeping with the contrariness of the Year 2000 problem, we can assure you that no matter which approach you prefer, you will find situations where it is best to use the other.

LET'S GET PHYSICAL

The two approaches differ in both time and cost. The primary difference is in whether you change the data. The logical approach retains the data in the format in which it currently exists. The physical approach requires you to change the data so that it contains four digits, including the two digits of the century.

When we first began to talk about fixing the Year 2000 problem years ago, we said that the only option was to change the data, thereby making the data accurate and reducing the number of design changes required. Think about it: If you compared two dates that both contained the century, you wouldn't have to worry about having to change most of the logic.

```
IF EXPIRATION-DATE < TODAYS-DATE THEN
```

When EXPIRATION-DATE equals 20000101 and TODAYS-DATE is 19991201, the process works fine, but if EXPIRATION-DATE equals 000101 and TODAYS-DATE is 991201, the comparison fails, and we have to insert logic to work with the dates.

If you change the data, then the typical processes of computing, sorting, locating, and comparing will continue to work without modification. Because less of the code is changed, there is a chance for less testing. If you reduce testing (typically three to four times the effort of changing code), then you save precious time, and code should function correctly until January 1 of Year 10000.

There is a price to pay, though. Changing the data means you have to write conversion programs and temporary "bridge" programs that create files in the old format to allow unchanged programs to read the data. This adds programming time and requires testing of programs. Writing these programs requires us to study the data and even fix it where the data is bad. Although these programs are not hard to write, and many code-generator programs make them relatively trivial, they still must be written and tested.

The insertion of bridges adds to the processing clock, making certain jobs run longer. And field expansion can add to the data storage requirements, necessitating more data storage media and even devices. Plus, screens and reports need to be changed, sometimes requiring redesign. There are ways of changing the data definitions so that both changed and unchanged programs can read the same data. The following is a COBOL example.

Where the original data definition is:

```
15 INDATE-YYMMDD.
  20 INDATE-YY  PIC X(02).
  20 INDATE-MM  PIC X(02).
  20 INDATE-DD  PIC X(02).
```

the data field could be expanded, and the revised file definition could be changed to read as follows:

```
15 INDATE-CCYYMMDD.
  20 INDATE-CCYY  PIC X(04).
  20 FILLER  PIC X(04).
15 INDATE-WITHCC REDEFINES INDATE-CCYYMMDD.
  20 FILLER  PIC X(02).
  20 INDATE-YYMMDD.
    25 INDATE-YY  PIC X(02).
    25 INDATE-MM  PIC X(02).
    25 INDATE-DD  PIC X(02).
```

It would then be necessary only to recompile the unchanged code to include the new file definition. The revised programs would use INDATE-CCYYMMDD in place of INDATE-YYMMDD, and INDATE-CCYY in place of INDATE-YY. These changes are easy to make with a program editor tool.

IT'S LOGICAL

If, however, you can retain the data as is, with only two digits for the year, you can save the cost of creating conversion programs, building bridges, and expanding the data storage space. You can even continue to ignore the bad data that might exist in your files (nobody noticed it before). Further, you won't have to worry about changes to screens and reports, where changes require interaction with the application user and modification to training, documentation, and speed of data entry.

You would start by adding logic to the programs, either by inserting vendor-supplied routines ("windows") that artificially and temporarily expand the date by supplying some implied century or by explicitly adding proprietary code to test the range of the years, as in "If date 1 > 50 and date 2 < 49 then . . ."

The two-digit, or logical, approach, requires more code redesign and thus more testing. Inserting the routines to supply the century information involves some programming and testing time. In situations where processing cycle time is critical, these additional instructions could alter the length of the computer run. These are the obvious penalties.

The less obvious problems come from several places. First, we are assuming that the processing of dates is correct in the first place and that the data is correct. Second, we believe we know the range of the dates in the files and that they can be handled by a single process. Third, we add to the complexity of the code, which means there is more opportunity for problems that will cause breakdowns in the future, thereby increasing maintenance costs. Dilemmas also arise when you consider how to enter and display data with only two digits. And data entry tends to be much more difficult, because whoever inputs data must start making decisions about it. Today, when a data-entry clerk receives a form that reads "990102" or "010299," he or she can safely assume that the month is January. But what happens on "010102"? Ambiguity. In the first 12 years of the century, without any obvious numerical way to distinguish between years and months, dates will be entered inconsistently, and errors will be much harder to spot and verify.

The same is true of displays. We saw a single report in England that displayed the date in the formats MMDDYY, YYMMDD, and the European standard DDMMYY. Needless to say, this caused major confusion. The only way to avoid such confusion is to change the way the data is displayed so that it is always presented in the same format.

There is no right answer, and both strategies entail compromises. Nevertheless, people *do* report an immediate benefit from retaining the two-digit-year format. Reports indicate a 20 to 30 percent reduction in the cost versus what they expected to pay if they made all the dates four digits. (Keep in mind that nobody does it both ways and gathers real statistics.) If you can achieve these savings, then retaining two-digit years is faster; and if time is short, with an impending event horizon, the choice is obvious.

PICK YOUR POISON

So what is the best solution? When the pressure is on to meet a date, your only option appears to be the logical approach; but you will be making the sacrifices mentioned. Over the long run, the physical approach costs less because the logical approach introduces more errors and depends on the use of a technique called *windowing,* which we will describe shortly. But "windows" do not work forever, and eventually have to be closed.

You will have to set your own priorities and then weigh the consequences. Again, you probably will have to make this decision for each application you change. To make the decision that is right for you, you need to evaluate the following factors for *each and every* application:

Time needed to change the code
Cost to change the code
Availability of resources to change the code or the data

Time and cost required to change the data

Time required to process the data

Amount of data to be changed

Cost of maintenance over time

Remember, no matter which option you choose, you cannot escape the cost of testing, which usually demands that you make trade-offs. There is still the problem of what do you do with "flags," bad date routines, unusual logic, and so on. Another reminder: Neither solution even attempts to deal with the less common date-formatting standards.

Windows, Bridges, and Wrappers

We referred to "windows" and "bridges" in the last section; here, we will describe them more fully. We'll add to the mix another popular technique for dealing with dates: using *wrappers*.

DOING WINDOWS

The windows method for dealing with dates comes in two forms: *fixed* and *sliding*. Both assume a 100-year period. A typical 100-year period is from 1950 to 2049. This might be used as a "fixed" window of time. A fixed window uses a base year that is dependent on the data. If, for instance, the data does not include a year prior to, say, 1984, you can set the base year at 1984. Then logic can be inserted that enables users to look at any year in the data and assign a century, based on the knowledge that for years between 84 and 99, the century prefix can be assumed to be 19. Subsequent logic in this example then assumes that any year from 00 to 83 can be assigned the century prefix 20.

If you take the current year and subtract 10 and determine the century (e.g., 1997 minus 10 is 1987), you can assume 87 to 99 has a century value of 19. Anything else has a century value of 20—an implied value.

This "sliding window" works well through 2010, *if* the old data is not kept longer than 10 years and nothing is entered incorrectly with 00, or until the data refers to the year 2087, where the century value is incorrectly implied. You could use a sliding window of 20, which then works well until 2020. Sliding windows are used only with data that is not intended to be retained for a long period of time. If you handle five-year subscriptions, for example, you know that no subscription will be in the file longer than six years; thus anything in the file will not be older than six years from the current date.

Although sliding windows appear safer because they apparently will adjust themselves, there is a problem with windows in general. Because there are many different dates stored in data, and each may have a different base year or retention period, it is possible that you might be unable to set a base year for all the date data in the program or even to use a sliding window. Chances are, the base date or duration of the sliding window will have to change several times. (We have seen as many as seven changes in a single program.) Therefore, you must be very careful in using windows.

Knowledge of the data is important, and the programs must be well documented so that those who change the code later understand the value of the window when a code change is processed. Not knowing the data can result in the placement of time bombs, which occur when the window logic fails. Many times they are difficult to detect and hard to resolve, and consequently can cause severe damage to data. Some enterprises have already suffered the penalties of making assumptions about their data.

BUILDING BRIDGES

Bridge programs read data in either the two-digit- or four-digit-year format and produce a file with the format of the year reversed. The two-digit year is changed to four. The four-digit to two. Another term popularly used for a limited bridge used to trap transactions is *filter*. Bridges (or filters) are inserted into processing routines where the data is read sequentially. Typically, a filter or bridge is placed between transaction entry, updates of master files, sorts, and merges. Bridges are also inserted when it is necessary to create a file that is used by another application.

In situations where the application is changed to use four-digit years, and the input from another application remains unchanged, a bridge is installed that regularly runs a conversion program that inserts century information in the date fields, creating a temporary file. Windows are often used in construction of such bridges. A single fixed window can be used to handle the determination of century for the bulk of the dates in the data. As long as it is possible to determine the earliest date stored, the window can provide the century. Obviously, this solution will not work if you have date ranges in a field greater than 100 years or dates that extend back or forward more than 99 years from the present year. For these you may need to write overrides to the century calculations.

In some cases, the use of a bridge may make it unnecessary to change an application—specifically, when the application is scheduled for replacement. A bridge program can feed two-digit information to that program until its event horizon is reached or until 2000. If a bridge is employed between one application and another that performs only "forward looks" at the data (that is, it does not reference historical information), the application may require only minimal changes. Forward-look applications do not perform operations that cannot be solved by inserting a single sliding window, with the current year as the base, in each of the programs.

Bridge programs are relatively easy to construct. Many programs that automatically alter the programs from two digits to four digits automatically produce a template that is used to construct a bridge. You use the two file formats—the old format with two-digit years and the new one with expanded date fields. The simple part involves providing instructions to pass all the nondate data from one file to the other. A window is turned on, and the date fields that fit the window ranges and are in the common format (character strings in the format of MMDDYY or YYMMDD) are moved. Fields that are being converted from one format to another (e.g., MMDDYY to YYYY-MMDD, YYMMDD to YYYYDDD, or from strings to packed-decimal or binary) can also be processed using the window. Turning off the window, the other date fields that cannot be processed through the window can be reformatted by special instructions.

Processing of this nature might include inserting century information based on logical relationships, converting end-of-file records, changing date stamps, and altering record key fields. An example of a logical relationship requirement might be found in a situation where an insurance policy is issued to someone whose birth year is 99 and whose parent's birthday is indicated by the value in the year of 55, in which case we could assume the century prefix for both to be 19. If, on the other hand, the child was born in 40 and the parent was born in 99, we would probably be correct in assuming the parent was born in 1899. We would then insert an 18 into the parent's century position. An end-of-file record might contain all 9s in the old records date field where the end-of-file record contains *high values*. We have seen key fields containing numeric years in two digits stripped of the date data and replaced with an alphanumeric sequence code.

The other type of bridge changes the date data from four-digit years to two-digit years. This might require that changes made by one application be reversed. Let's assume that every program in one application has already been altered to use century information (e.g., YYYYMMDD, YYYYDDD) and may or may not be stored in a different mode (e.g., binary versus character). This data is used elsewhere in the same applications or is passed to another application containing programs that are unprepared to use the dates with century expansion. The new format is as follows:

```
05 INDATE.
    10 INDATE-CCYY       PIC 9999.
    10 INDATE-MM         PIC 99.
    10 INDATE-DD         PIC 99.
05 INTERM.
    10 INTERM-CODE       PIC XX.
    10 INTERM-PERCENT    PIC V99.
```

Compare to the old format:

```
05 INDATE.
    10 INDATE-MM         PIC XX.
    10 INDATE-DD         PIC XX.
    10 INDATE-YY         PIC XX.
05 INTERM REDFINES INDATE.
    10 INTERM-CODE       PIC XXXX.
    10 INTERM-PERCENT    PIC V99.
```

The unchanged application expects MMDDYY in the old mode, which may have allowed the date field to contain nondate data stored in the field (INTERM). One or more conversion routines are needed. The first routine would look to see if the INTERM data was stored in the incoming expanded date record, translate the INTERM-CODE from new to old, and move it to the output record in the old format. A second routine would change the sequence of date data and store it in the output record. The routine would take the input date in the mode in which it exists and create the output date in the mode that is expected, stripping the leading digits from the year field. In other cases, routines may be required to perform compression, decompression, or conversion from Gregorian to Julian/ordinal or Julian/ordinal to Gregorian.

Under Wrappers

Wrappers are a relatively new solution to date-processing problems. A wrapper usually has many components, which surround a computer process to trap the inputs and the outputs. There are two types of wrappers. The first is inserted directly into the program; the second is installed in the job process control and is sometimes called an *envelope*.

Wrappers are inserted into the code in both old and newly reformatted programs so that they can share the data concurrently. The wrapper corrects old date data or reverses new date data as it is read. An example of a typical program wrapper presented at seminars by Peritus Software Services, Inc., follows.

Old program

```
READ INPUT-MSTR INTO POLICY
        AT END...
        NOT AT END...
END-READ
WRITE OUT-MSTR FROM POLICY
```

New program

```
CALL "WR-READ-INPOLICY-RECORD"
    IF AT END > 0...
    IF AT END < 0...
END-READ
CALL "WR-WRITE-OUTPOLICY-RECORD"
```

In this example, the new program's read routine would either insert century information or eliminate century information using a process similar to that explained in the discussion of bridges. Such routines are often used in transaction processing where screens and reports may not have enough space to handle the display of four-digit years.

Envelopes are used when there is no time to make the changes required to an application, or when the hardware does not handle the Year 2000 dates. An envelope is a "time machine" that makes the application function as if it were running 28 years ago! The system date in the machine is set back 28 years, thus extending the life of the equipment.

Creating either type of wrapper requires identification of all the date fields to a program or programs being run in a job stream. An input wrapper program is invoked when a job is started. The first type often is inserted by changing the program control language instructions to run the input wrapper component before the first program is run. This program reads the input files and changes the date fields. The job may require an internal wrapper for transaction input that intercepts on-line interaction and changes the dates before they are received by the program. The transaction wrapper component is usually inserted as a call in the processing program.

As noted, the wrapper program is much like a bridge program. The programmer is required to provide the code to change each date field. Often, windows are employed to assign the correct century prefix in the arithmetic activity. The input wrapper used in an envelope finds all the dates on the input files, and subtracts a specific number of years (28) from all dates in the files, or an intercepted on-line entry transaction. (If the year being looked at is 00, the window tells the program that it is 2000. Subtracting 28 returns a value of 72, which is written over the 00 on the file.) The wrapper, in essence, rolls the clock back 28 years.

The use of the number 28 is not arbitrary. It is required to keep the days of the week aligned with the calendar for the current year. The wrapper contains the logical operations to deal with the years 1901 through 2099 effectively. Since the years 1900 and 2100 are not leap years, the 28-year rule breaks down, and the days of the week no longer line up.

The second part of an envelope collects all the output and reverses the process—adding 28 years to the dates. There might be many components to the output portion of the wrapper: one dealing with files, another with reports, and still another with interactive messages back to on-line users.

Be careful about where and how you apply and test wrappers. Messing with dates can become a legal liability if not handled correctly. We suggest you do not use wrappers where you are altering customer-, investor-, or employee-related data. The advantage to wrappers is that they can be time-savers. Some organizations are changing all read and write processes to use wrappers. They indicate to the wrapper, by a constant in the data definition portion or the program, whether the program is millennium-compliant. The wrapper can thus be used permanently, unlike bridges, after all the programs have been converted.

GETTING AND USING WINDOWS, BRIDGES, AND WRAPPERS

Windows, bridges, and wrappers can be built or bought. IBM, for example, has included windows as part of its latest release of COBOL. An increasing number of sort routines are being offered with the capability of windowing so that two-digit year designations can be retained without redefining sort parameters. Sort parameters refer to the positions in the physical data transfer where the date field begins and ends.

Some of the newest rule-based date-conversion programs generate skeleton code for bridges and data-conversion programs. Combined with a proprietary library of subroutines to execute century insertions, the creation of bridges and data-conversion programs can take minutes instead of hours. Further, new code-conversion programs may be able to install a wrapper in the program that is generated.

The pricing of these tools varies widely. For instance, Prince Software sells its mainframe conversion tool Translate 2000 for about

$70,000. A version running on a PC called MicroFocus Revolve sells for about $10,000 for a 25-workstation license (Revolve is about $3,000 per workstation). Prices change frequently. Service providers change the code for a per-line rate. Current prices are very high— about three times what they should be according to estimates of the per-line rate and the effort being saved. If the estimate is, for example, $1.50 per line for the total, the cost of the change should be about 8 to 12 percent. This means the cost should be $.12 to $.18. But expect to pay $.50. However, the price should drop rapidly as more services come on-line.

Using windows, bridges, and wrappers effectively and efficiently will, of course, be a management challenge. No matter which of these tools you implement, you will have to keep track of what you implement and where. If yours is an environment in which documentation is only a "sometime thing," using these tools is risky.

Installing and uninstalling also requires tracking where to put them and when to get rid of them. Many such organizations are finding it necessary to build special programs to track where bridges, wrappers, and windows have been installed. Bridges are the easiest to track. If you can determine that all the jobs, applications, and exports that use a bridge have been made century-compliant, you can remove it. For windows, we recommend keeping track of the type of window and, for fixed windows, the date range. We suggest that you anticipate using wrappers if you are building a tracking tool.

To Test or Not to Test

We have discussed the importance of testing throughout the book, and the enormity of time it will take—from 40 to 50 percent of the entire update project. Not testing is not an option, but as time runs short (as it already has) there are some places where you might be forced to forgo the testing procedure.

Run down your list of applications: Evaluate those that are necessary for your enterprise's survival, those that are required for you to remain competitive, those that make you a market leader, those that provide information, and finally, those that reduce workloads. Only you can determine whether you will allow yourself to be "forced" not to test. Remember as you evaluate all this that the testing load is enormous for critical applications. You will want to perform the following:

- *Complete test script development* for all date processes
- *Baseline testing,* to ascertain that all dates between now and the Year 2000 are handled correctly
- *Unit testing,* to assure that design changes and windows work for dates from the Year 2000 for each program that is changed
- *String testing,* to make sure that data is sorted correctly and passed from program to program within a job, or from platform to platform within an import or export process
- *Systems testing,* to determine that daily, weekly, and other time-dependent processes work correctly
- *Integration testing,* to determine whether data bridges and other interfaces between applications work as predicted
- *Acceptance testing,* to prove to an application's client/user that all changes are working as planned and the program is ready to be returned to production
- *Parallel testing,* to give users time to acclimate to changes, and to make sure that critical processing works through period-ending cycles (quarter and year-end processing)
- *Regression testing,* to determine whether changes to feeder applications have not altered processing or introduced errors

Forgoing testing is never acceptable, but in the real world, it happens. More than one enterprise has decided not to perform unit and string testing, in the belief that if the application can meet a set of high-level criteria for century compliance as part of a systems test, then it can be returned to production. Further, the thinking goes, if failures subsequently occur in production, they will probably not be of such difficulty to fix that the application must be out of production for a significant length of time.

In a somewhat similar vein, some enterprises have decided that any applications that do not yet deal with dates beyond year 1999 be reintroduced to production without any testing, with the intention that the application support teams will provide testing during a normal release cycle. And when applications are not involved with extending or maintaining competitive advantage, you must consider putting them back into production without testing. But forewarned is forearmed: If these applications fail, they will increase the workload and force decisions about how to spend your resources.

So what do you test for? The best guidelines shared in public to date in this regard are provided by GTE and reproduced here.

Category	Subcategory	Guidelines
General	Current date	• Direct set, power-up rollover
		• Reinitialize from cold start
		• Full date ranges
	Calendar accuracy	• Days of week in 2000 and 2001
		• Leap year in 2000
		• 366 days in 2000; 365 in 2001
	Century ambiguity	• High-risk values (1999-09-09, 1999-12-31, 1900-01-01, 2000-01-01, 2000-02-29, 2000-03-01)
		• Ambiguous century in user interface
		• Electronic interfaces (e.g., system date)
Technology-specific	Current date	• Power-down continuity
		• System date versus current date
	Date representation	• Overflow of base-and-offset representation
		• Standards for Gregorian and ordinal date formats
		• Century capability in storage and interfaces *(continues)*

Category	Subcategory	Guidelines
	Date manipulation	• Date arithmetic
		• Conversion between representations
		• Sorting, searching, indexing
		• Century designation available in storage and interfaces
Domain-specific	Century ambiguity	• Accuracy in inferring century for each field in storage, user interface, and other interfaces
	Date representation	• Industry standards and contract requirements
		• Human factors requirements
		• Design and coding standards
	Date manipulation	• Access to archived data
		• Manipulation of archived data
		• Extended semantics

We feel that a complete testing process should evaluate the applications handling of the following years: 1900, 1980, 1996, 1998, 1999, 2000, 2001, 2002, 2004, 2020, 2028, 2032, and 2038. Testing should consider the following period rollovers:

- End-of-day (with special consideration of 08-Sep-1999)
- End-of-week: last week, this week, next week
- End-of-month: last month, this month, next month
- End of bimonthly period
- End-of-quarter: last quarter, this quarter, next quarter
- End-of-season/semester/etc.
- End-of-year: last year, this year, next year
- Leap year

There should also be testing of date conversions from Gregorian to ordinal/Julian and ordinal/Julian to Gregorian. (For those who wonder about the ordinal/Julian notation, the difference between the two is that the ordinal day starts at midnight, while the Julian day starts at noon.) Also test any conversions from ASCII to EBCDIC and back. Test for the application's ability to handle the following values in date fields: low values, high values, all 9s, and all 0s.

We do not recommend forgoing testing to anyone involved with applications that interface directly with the public. Nor should you skip unit testing for applications required for you to maintain your competitive position. We recommend that if you are forced to curtail testing, you always make sure that whoever is responsible for the application monitors it.

Clearly, untested changes create vulnerable applications. The future does offer hope, though. A number of tool developers are working on a process based on application reengineering capabilities that identify the critical testing processes in an application and execute a statistics-based test on those processes to determine whether they will fail. Such tools could short-circuit the need for manual testing, at least for language-specific applications. But until they are available, and certainly where multiple languages are used, expect to test, test, test.

Chapter Eight

Taking a Tool Inventory

When we start a millennium update project at a new client site, often one of these two scenarios is in progress: Either the client has too few software tools to support code development and maintenance, or the client has too many tools. Where there are too few tools, they may be used and misused for multiple purposes; where there are too many tools, they may be poorly understood or used at cross-purposes. It is difficult to say which situation is worse, but it is safe to say that most organizations have acquired tools without a plan, or have integrated them poorly to support their application development and maintenance effort.

When there are no tools, there are also no processes in place to identify requirements, locate vendors, assess tools, train and coach the staff, integrate the tools into the current development or maintenance process, or manage the tools. In too many instances, enterprises do not have a budget for buying software tools, or there is resistance to purchasing tools because there is nothing in place to substantiate productivity claims or prove a return on investment. An enterprise in this state has to find help from the outside to provide the required services and some degree of assurance to management that purchases will be cost-justified.

On the other hand, such an enterprise does not have the problem of one that has been aggressive in purchasing tools. Such enterprises often have a toolbox full of "shelfware"—tools that have fallen into disuse, assuming they were ever properly introduced. The problem is that information technology organizations don't really know what they own. Their tools are not tracked like plant equipment: They usually are not capitalized or depreciated; they are not associated with a business function (do you know anyone who puts IT in the category of a business?), so the tools expense is treated as overhead.

We have also seen enterprises that owned tools that performed identical functions on the same hardware and operating system platform. In such situations, loyalty to the tools has become an ease-of-use issue: The group devoted to one tool refuses to use another simply because of the retraining and familiarization costs.

Consequently, when we get major corporations ready to analyze, classify, plan, prepare, convert, and reintegrate date-sensitive applications, we find that first we must make them understand that using an effective toolkit is the starting point. If you recognized your organization in one of the preceding descriptions, our first suggestion is that you take a tool inventory. Most organizations fall woefully short when they examine their inventory in relationship to the tasks that need to be supported for the millennium update. (In the next chapter, we discuss the types of tools that you may want to use in addressing the date problem.) That you will need effective tools to process and update your applications is not debatable, because even with maximum tool implementation, industry cost estimates are alarming, but they are even higher without the effective use of tools.

Hand Me the Wrench

The tool inventory requires capturing two kinds of information. The first category is information about tool ownership; the second has to do with potential use of tools in the process. Taking stock of what you have and where it will be used will identify gaps in your tool-box. Whether you should fill those gaps will require some difficult decision making. A complete tool inventory will have four separate deliverables:

Tool inventory list: tools owned and their current status
Tool requirements: processes to be performed during the update
Gap analysis: tools to be purchased (or built) with an estimate of benefit
Tool acquisition and assimilation plan: tools to buy, and when and how to implement them

TOOL INVENTORY LIST

Start your inventory with the operating system environment. Many hardware vendors provide a number of tools with the operating system, such as code library management tools, date routines, and special sort processes to handle the sorting of two-digit years across the century boundary.

Your second source of information about what you own should be the programmers and analysts. In many cases, they use internally built tools, and determining what they are may reveal that some of them could be of use to others. The most common internally built tools include date routines and data analysis tools.

The third place to look for tools is with your purchasing agent. Some tools may have been purchased and subsequently forgotten. We found one end-user organization had purchased and installed three tools that were of use in the update project, but the computer professionals were not even aware they were on the computers they used every day. (The computer operations and technical support staff who maintain the systems software bought them and never shared the information with the programmers.)

As you locate tools, determine the following:

- *Version being used.* Is the latest version installed? If it is not, you may find that other actions must be taken before the tool can be employed in the update process. You may discover that the tool has not been maintained because the service contract was not purchased, the number of users is too small, or operating system software has not been brought up to the level required.

- *Functions performed.* Some tools perform more than one function. In the next chapter, we will discuss the functions to look for. For now, just determine whether the tool serves more than one function so you do not buy another tool unnecessarily. In some cases, you will find that the label applied to the function is not consistent with industry definitions. Many vendors strive to create an image of uniqueness, but do not actually achieve it. Investigate to ascertain what the advertised functions really provide.

- *Platform characteristics required.* Information on the hardware model, operating system, computer languages, and other characteristics of the tool will tell you whether you have duplicate tools or tools that perform duplicate functions on other platforms. If you work off several platforms or in multiple computer languages, you may need to acquire several tools of similar functions.

- *Date use.* Some tools contain date processes, which may cause some difficulty with a tool if it is not date-compliant. For example, you may not be able to use one in an environment where you are simulating running in Year 2000 or later. Watch for data storage processes that include date stamping. This can make the data unusable from run to run when the system date changes. Test any such tool if the vendor cannot provide you with a clear answer.

- *Support from vendor.*   Like application software products, many tools have changed ownership over the last five years. In some cases, this has improved tool support and included integration of the tool into a suite. You may find improved support through "hot lines," e-mail, or new and electronic training media. Or you may find that the original support has declined as the number of tool users has decreased, providing less income for support maintenance. Even when a tool is in frequent use by the technical staff, reassess support. And do not overlook a review of your maintenance agreement. You will want to know the response you are entitled to if the operating system has changed or the tool is sold.

- *Usage of the tool.*   Whether a tool was purchased (in use or not) or built, determine its skill requirements, training time, training requirements (manuals, formal classes, coaching, laboratories, etc.), number and location of users, and problems with or limitations to use. Again, this information will be important when you make decisions about implementation. A staff tool-skills matrix may come in handy—you will find that some staff members make maximum use of tools while others do not. The former may be candidates for the "tiger teams" discussed in the previous chapter.

- *Attitudes.*   When performing tools inventories, it is essential to determine both the technologists' and the management's attitude toward tools; this is part of a context assessment. Some organizations have set up hidden roadblocks to tool purchase and implementation. Examples of these include lack of training facilities, inadequate training or travel budgets, imposition of inflexible due dates, and failure to acknowledge tools use. In some cases, there is hostility on the part of management to tools use, arising from ignorance of what the tool will do to improve performance, or from a fear of reprisals if the tool is not implemented correctly. In such business cultures, tool use cannot thrive. A context assessment can prove invaluable in putting together recommendations for purchases and implementation.

◆ *Creating an environment.*   A tool tends to be "owned" by the organization that acquires it. In large, decentralized organizations, this causes pockets of advocates for various tools. It also makes it exceedingly difficult for other staff units to use or share the tool. This may be due to funding issues—maintenance comes out of one group's budget even though others may use it. The difficulty in sharing tools may also be a result of support issues: It is natural for new users to look to experienced users for help. When the support is departmentally linked, but not enterprisewide, new users can't get the help they need. Review your organization context and define the tools environment. This may lead to recommendations for creating a tools "owner" who manages all the tools, training, and support.

Automate or Extricate

Experience has taught that automation is only as good as the process. Tools become "shelfware" when they are bought before the process is defined. Two things must be present before a tool is used: repetitive tasks and frequent use. If a task is not performed the same way *every* time, it cannot be automated. Where exceptions to a process are encountered more than 20 percent of the time, tool users will abandon the tool. Similarly, if users do not invoke the tool frequently enough, they may require a reeducation process, which, if it lasts more than 20 minutes, may discourage use and result in rejection of the tool.

These conditions for tool rejection can be avoided only by having a well-defined process in place. This process should include requirements for use of the tool, steps to intercept and deal with nonstandard situations prior to requiring the tool's use, organizing the work

so that those trained to use the tool do so regularly, and measurement and metrics relating to the tool and the task.

If, however, you are well into problem resolution and predefining
is not possible, there are some effective ways to determine your tools
requirements. Having enumerated your application and tools inventories, you are already aware that you have to deal with a complex
environment, including some or all of the following:

Multiple hardware platforms
Different operating systems
Several data management processes and packages
Multiple computer languages
Several versions or extensions to those languages
Code generators, query tools, and report writers
Automated and manual event-driven actions

These factors, which will determine your tools requirements, fall
into two categories: core update processes and project processes. The
first category includes those tools used to perform technical work.
Update processes include such tasks as code and data analysis, program and data changes, and testing. Project processes include management of code and resources, estimation, measurement, change
control, and methodology or process management.

Project administration tools are essential to managing the project. Centralized programs will find tools that enable defining tasks
and tracking progress so that you can identify the impact of changes
in plans and schedules. Although you may normally plan and track
projects in your head, don't even consider doing so for this project.
Many sophisticated planning tools cannot handle a complete plan for
an enterprise that manages 4 million lines of code. Usually, the plan
has to be broken up and handled in pieces. Fortunately, project management tools abound, and many enterprises employ two or three
PC-based tools.

Another important project tool is a *repository.* But most enterprises do not have a repository, and those that do find their contents do not reflect the current state of the external application data. A good repository tracks all the components in the environment and their status; it provides information on relationships among components so that plans to implement a change to one component will reveal potential change requirements for other components. Configuration management tools perform some elements of this function, but a true repository will capture relationships that include components such as vendor software, hardware, embedded systems, regulations, imports and exports of data, and test scripts and test data. The problem with repositories is that their contents must be loaded without automated input mechanisms, and creation of the contents, called *metadata,* is a major task.

Core tools will be useful, but depend on the work to be done. The following is a breakdown of the types of core tools to consider for each stage of the project. A more complete discussion of these tools follows in Chapter 9.

• **Portfolio inventory and estimation**

Scanners or parsers: Tools that look for dates to determine whether code has to be changed and assess the level of work required.

Estimators: Tools that forecast the effort required, the cost, and the duration.

• **Update planning**

Documentation aids: Tools that recover information on software functions from software code.

Source recovery: Tools/services that can re-create source code from machine language instructions if the source is lost. Several tools are available for purchase.

Workflow analysis: Tools that describe and diagram workflows and workflow requirements for input and skills.

♦ **Update preparation**

Scanners/parsers: Tools that find every reference to dates and date processing so that design problems can be uncovered.

Data analyzers: Tools that look through data to uncover problems such as nondate data stored in date fields, illogical dates, use of date constants, dates stored in fields not defined as dates, and so on.

♦ **Code and data change**

Editors: Tools that allow manual changes to code.

Conversion aids: Tools that upgrade language versions or allow code to be run on another platform.

Intelligent editors: Tools that automatically expand data definitions to four digits and make predefined changes based on rules to date processes.

Syntax checkers and static analyzers: Tools that look for logical inconsistencies in changed code.

Code generators: Tools that assist in the construction of bridges or data-conversion programs.

Data generators: Tools that produce test data based on rules provided by the operator.

Dynamic test analyzers and debuggers: Tools that track the process steps and capture and display the status of fields during testing; some provide test coverage analysis to show which parts of a program were tested and which were not.

On-line simulators: Tools that mimic the entry of test data from terminals.

Date simulators: Tools that cause programs to behave as if they were being run in a different time.

Data migration aids: Tools that transfer data from one file to another and view that process.

Code comparators: Tools that show differences in source code from version to version.

Gap Analysis

A gap analysis is performed to determine the differences between your current state and where you want to be. It is the time to open a discussion regarding any and all tools issues, to recommend actions to promote tools use, or to overcome resistance to tools. If, for example, a tool exists as shelfware and is generally regarded by staff as unusable, the particulars should be enumerated during the gap analysis. If staff skill sets are not up to par, this is the forum in which to reveal that fact and to decide whether you need a tool trainer, a tool manager, or someone to design processes to employ automated tools.

Specifically, for the millennium update project, the processes to implement and employ the tools will have to be delineated *before* you can identify the tools you need to build or purchase. Simply put, until your processes are defined, the specific requirements for tools cannot be known. While performing your gap analysis, we generally recommend that specific tools not be itemized; instead, identify a number of tools that fit your general requirements. These can be used to provide a range of costs to do your budget estimations. Specific tool recommendations should be made only in the following three circumstances:

- You wish to resurrect a shelfware product or promote an internally developed tool, in which case, you should include specific recommendations about how to reintroduce the tool for general use.
- You decide to build a tool because of proprietary coding requirements.
- You already own tools that are part of a vendor's tool suite and can obtain significant advantage by using another tool in that suite.

A gap analysis should also include the funding requirements for tools, training, process development, tools management, vendor liaison and software maintenance, staff coaching, help-desk support, and supplemental software purchases.

Outside services can perform a gap analysis for you. Data Dimensions, for example, has been performing such services since 1992. It has an extremely large database on tools, and their process often takes less than three weeks. This is often much faster than a similar procedure can be organized by an enterprise. Internally supported studies often do not have the same resources, and options may be much narrower simply because there is little time to do the research. In a large organization in which many tools are owned, there is also severe pressure from advocates of certain tools which slows down decision making.

A good gap analysis from an outside provider will assess the return on tools purchased. This will most likely be estimated based on the difference between doing the update with tools versus doing it without. These are subjective evaluations based on prior experience of the company performing the gap analysis.

USE 'EM OR LOSE 'EM

We are often asked by millennium update clients: "How much should I spend on tools?" The answer, of course, has to do with your understanding of the role tools play in the project. Simply buying tools will not solve the problem; you must also plan for introduction, testing, training, and integration. Some medium-size enterprises have established a fund of $500,000 to $750,000 to buy tools and training. This amount represents from 5 to 10 percent of the estimated cost of the update—this, of course, assumes the maximum use of tools.

The purpose of buying tools is to reduce work and/or cycle time. Certain tasks are virtually impossible to accomplish without tools—

scanning for dates, for example. Some activities can obtain up to a 40 percent reduction in effort through the use of a tool—for instance, code changes. Again, any measurable benefit depends on the knowledge and skill of the tool user. The average savings on effort is probably around 37 percent. (A helpful comparison: If your change process is estimated to cost the equivalent of 15 person-years, a savings of this magnitude may amount to more than five person-years. The average fully burdened rate in the United States is $100,000 per year. You could easily buy a tool suite for a third of the savings.) Cycle time reduction is significantly affected by management processes, but a well-managed team can achieve an estimated 55 percent improvement in throughput as a result of adopting some tools.

Probably the most difficult question to answer is where in the process to begin to spend money on tools. Most enterprises currently spend slightly more than 40 percent of the update effort on testing and 20 percent on management of the process. We therefore recommend that if you do not have tools to support those two activities, you start there. If, however, you decide to farm out the work to a code-change service, perhaps you should spend your budget on analysis tools so you can better define your change requirements and test the solution that is provided. If you have to move your code to another version or platform, recover source code from machine language code, or work around a failing vendor product, your purchases are predefined, in the sense that you will need products designed to assist you in reengineering. Companies such as ViaSoft, Regnisys, Reasoning Systems, and Progeni, to name just a few, will be able to provide tools that help in design recovery, database migration, and language conversion tools.

Some tools provide some less-tangible benefits. Chief among these are improvements in product quality and application information. A repository, for instance, can lead the way to better control and management of the entire process of systems development and maintenance. Akin to the repository is what we call a *relationship map-*

per, a tool that will search for components and establish immediate relationships.

What is missing in most enterprises today is an up-to-date and complete knowledge of all the relationships that exist between components. It is difficult to research the linkages between programs, system software dependencies, data, shared code members, control language sets, other applications that use the data, and so on. This makes it difficult to estimate the true impact of change on the entire organization. When one component changes, it often causes a ripple effect, requiring changes in other applications; and we often don't realize that until it's too late. Unfortunately, a tool that constantly queries the environment and maintains the list of dependencies has yet to be developed. Those that are available require the user to keep the data up-to-date.

Code processing tools are invaluable aids when trying to determine what to test and the path that date information follows within a program or an application. Language parsers can provide dynamic documentation of code so that functionality can be tested and new requirements documented accurately with less effort. Analysis tools can prevent unnecessary decay of code quality, which leads to higher maintenance costs.

THE LEARNING CURVE

Which tools you purchase should not be just a dollars-and-cents decision. Don't forget to factor in people issues before introducing tools: Individual capabilities for learning differ; only a limited number of tools can be assimilated at one time; and the duration of the tool's learning cycle can vary.

How successfully tools are introduced depends on how quickly any one individual becomes comfortable and competent with a tool. Nevertheless, certain assumptions can be made for an entire organization. Generally, a relatively simple tool (having a single function with a familiar interface) requires two weeks of training and implementation; a complex tool (one that performs multiple functions) requires four weeks of use to reach the comfort zone. Competency, the point at which the tool starts to recover cost, is usually not achieved until several weeks after comfort is achieved. A second tool should not be introduced until the comfort zone on the first has been reached.

Our experience indicates that it can take up to six months for people to achieve proficiency with a complex tool. The impact of learning an additional tool is related to the level of success achieved in implementing the first. Simply, if the first is embraced enthusiastically, the second tool probably will be, too. If the tool performs an unrelated activity, the amount of time to achieve competency with either of them is lengthened.

In general, do not expect to implement a large number of tools; and those that you do choose to incorporate should be introduced first to staff members who are already familiar with using tools, as they will be more open to the learning process and thus be able to assimilate the knowledge faster. Choose carefully, because some tools require more effort. Configuration management tools, as pointed out earlier, are very difficult to install. Many enterprises have worked unsuccessfully for years to introduce such a tool, so if one isn't already in place, the millennium update project is not the time to add it. Other tools to avoid, because of the learning investment, include CASE tools, new 4GLs or code generators, data dictionaries, and a centralized project management system.

The success of a tool's integration into an organization is greatly amplified when there is someone to champion the tool and encourage others in its use. And having someone to troubleshoot minimizes frustration during the learning process. Consider retaining someone from the vendor as coach; or you may be able to recruit experienced help from a consulting service.

BUYER BEWARE

We caution you not to overspend on tools. Specifically, don't be swayed, for instance, by *intelligent editors,* those with the least competition and the most glitz, and regarded by many as the silver bullet. You'll even see them advertised as Year 2000 "solutions." They are not. They simply apply rules to the code and make changes. But beware: If the code doesn't fit the rule exactly, such tools may apply the change incorrectly, thus causing additional problems.

Use intelligent editors just as you would any other editor. This means knowing the rules that are being employed, analyzing the code, making design changes to fit the editing process, then—and only then—letting the editor do its thing. Ultimately, the tool is performing a rather small amount of work, so don't pay a high price.

PLATFORM TOOLING

Not all tools are available for all environments (*environment* here is defined as including the computer model, operating system, database management software, and communications and programming languages.) Certain environments simply do not have a large enough base to attract a large number of tool builders. IBM VM, Unisys 2200, and HP 1000 are all processors with limited support from the tool-building community, and few tools support languages like PL/1 or FORTRAN. In some cases, only the hardware manufacturer provides tools. HP 3000, Honeywell GECOS, and Data General fall into this category for their non-UNIX platforms. In general, more tools are designed for the most common environments.

Not surprisingly, then, the largest number of tools exist for IBM 360/370 architecture, using the MVS operating system with IMS and DB2 for data management, and either IMS/DC or CICS for communications. As for languages, COBOL has the most tools. At the other end of the scale are the low-volume platforms built for niche markets. Tandem, Data General, and Sun Microsystems platforms fit this profile. There are also tools available for multiple environments, an attractive option because all the tools have a similar user interface. Users who become proficient with the tool in one environment can more easily move to another.

Along the same line are tool suites, in development by many vendors. These tools, too, have common interfaces, and may work off a shared data collection file, making it possible to introduce several tools at roughly the same time. Usually it is cheaper to buy the suite than to purchase individual components. The downside is that you may have to uninstall a popular tool in favor of implementing the suite, so be prepared for some resistance if you find yourself in this situation.

An increasing number of tools that interface with multiple platforms also are being designed to run on a PC. This may be advantageous for a variety of reasons: Many platforms do not have sufficient capacity to support production, ongoing maintenance support, *and* a concurrent update project. In many cases, the need to alter the system date makes it difficult to schedule testing time. In addition, it may be necessary to add storage to some platforms (an additional cost) and require floor space that is not available. Thus, working off a PC offers several benefits:

- *Availability and extensibility.* More PCs can be added as required.
- *Storage.* PC storage capability and capacity is mounting rapidly.
- *Portability.* It is possible to acquire PCs that run mainframe software so that testing environments can be constructed outside of the production environment.
- *Tools.* Many tools are being developed that interface with several different platforms. Code and data can be moved to the PC environment, changed, tested, and moved back to the production environment with few or no differences in process.

- *Ease of use.* PC-based tools tend to be easier to learn and use. The capability to build and employ graphical and intuitive interfaces makes them easier to install. Progress with operating systems is also reducing learning time.

New tools that reduce testing requirements and improve project support on the PC are evolving; watch for them.

One word of caution, though, regarding PC tools: Do not underestimate the impact of introducing PCs if you have not already adopted them in your environment. They require new skill sets and building new communications to provide data transfer; and some routines will have to be recoded to work on the PCs.

Conclusion

We firmly believe that an effective suite of tools is essential to application development and maintenance. With the vast amount of code to be analyzed and updated, effective tools are mandatory for the completion of the millennium update. Keep in mind that all the competing technologies, vendors, and environments necessitate an understanding of the tools requirements, a plan for their introduction and use, and a well-trained staff to make them effective.

Chapter Nine

2000: A Tool Odyssey

In Chapters 1 and 8 we introduced the types of tools most directly associated with updating application code for the Year 2000, benefits to be derived from implementing such tools, and selection implications. In this chapter we examine the tools relevant to the millennium update project by type (we do not, however, name specific tools; such a discussion is beyond the scope of this book).

The number of available tools relevant to the millennium update is expanding rapidly, and we expect the total to exceed 3,000 before the deadline arrives. Obviously, there will be a ready market for any tool promising to improve productivity, but as we cautioned in Chapter 8, you must be wary of any tool offers that make unrealistic promises relating to the Year 2000 conversion effort. Throughout this period of tool development we expect prices to rise even though competition may be strong. Rising labor costs for development and support will force development and support costs upward. Platform-specific tools will become available for many environments that are tool-poor at present; but their prices will be especially high, reflecting their manufacturer's objective to recover development costs from fewer unit sales. These tools may come with

little or no support, but the benefit may be worth the investment
and the risk.

A number of Year 2000 "salvation" tools are already appearing
on the market; over 100 are now being sold with some version of
the words "Year 2000" attached to their name. A few are well
thought out, but many are just older tools with a few minor features
added to catch the wave of purchases by anxious buyers. A few are
being produced by people who have only a peripheral understanding
of the date change problems, and many of these are low-priced.
Remember the adage "you get what you pay for" here, because the
distributors of these low-priced products know that desperate managers will throw a relatively small amount of money at a product
they hope will work.

Bringing Method to the Madness

We discuss building a process using methodologies first, since
methodologies provide the rationale for the use of all the other tools.
Without a repeatable process—a method—work is difficult to automate and a tool may be ill-used or useless. People using tools seldom
achieve proficiency.

PRIMARY FUNCTION

You start by installing a process. Whenever we say this, most people
immediately think of a one-size-fits-all commercial methodology;
then they start to laugh because probably the most important and
least-used project tool most firms have invested in is a methodology. Computing development methodologies have been around
nearly as long as "computer programmer" has been a job title. Few
organizations have successfully implemented them. Most method-

ologies have played their most prominent role as placeholders on bookshelves.

So let's get our terms straight right from the start: A *methodology* is a collection of methods applied across the system's development life cycle. A *method* is a highly structured process for developing a specific product. It tells the user what to do in a step-by-step manner and, in some instances, offers specific instructions on creating a product defined by the method.

Methodologies differ in their degree of detail, tailorability, the amount of automation support, and the linkage to actual processes. At one end of the spectrum you will find rigid processes that define a step-by-step solution. At the other end, you will find highly flexible collections of modifiable processes designed to be adapted. Most of those used by consulting firms are biased by the kinds of work they were originally developed to support. Because they were designed to be used by consultants who constantly have to obtain approvals, they often do not fit the fast-paced process employed by an internal team. Most are written for software development and provide only minimal direction on maintenance. More than a few suggest that maintenance is similar to development, just requiring fewer steps.

Methodologies *do* provide definitions of products at each step and trace the work as it flows through the process, which can be extremely helpful because of the communication requirements of the Year 2000 activities. Further, methodologies often identify quality assurance steps and practices, suggesting where and when they are performed. They frequently provide forms and product examples and suggest techniques. Some enterprises' standards programs—which define procedures covering communications, project management, quality assurance, and change management—provide standards for some products, such as code or project reports, and effectively constitute a methodology. This is achieved when they strictly define the organization process flow and the format and content of acceptable deliverables.

YEAR 2000 RELEVANCE

When creating a Year 2000 "factory process," one that will enable high-quality and assembly-line conversion of code and implementation, it is helpful to start with a well-defined methodology. Put bluntly, you will not be able to succeed without a factory, and that requires a process!

Although, as just defined, methodologies often are organized as a step-by-step process, they do not have to be employed that way. Rather, a methodology should be viewed as a checklist or set of requirements. You can select the pieces that fit the process you need, tailor the description of the work to accommodate what has to be done, and then describe how to do it *in your organization.*

IDIOSYNCRASIES

Most commercial methodologies prescribe a single "right" way for developing applications, and thus lack the flexibility required to meet changes in cultural and organizational requirements. A number of them are supported by programmed routines that communicate to planning tools (discussed shortly). We believe that the more pragmatic the methodology, the more likely it is to have a project management tool interface. We have found that the tool interface makes the methodology more palatable, but structural inflexibility remains a problem.

Nevertheless, new methodologies that specifically address the reengineering of existing applications, and the Year 2000 problem in particular, have found a ready market in enterprises seeking guidance in an information-poor environment. As with all tools, expect methodologies to evolve and mature as they are used. Before acquiring a methodology, do some research to identify one that is built on a strong experience base in fixing the Year 2000 problem. You will find these to be maintenance-oriented and not grounded in software reengineering or development.

STAFFING IMPACT

Handled properly, implementing a methodology will have a beneficial impact on staff productivity, as it will require examination of current practices. A methodology provides a starting point for creating process definitions and a common vocabulary for describing the work.

Most methodologies are difficult to implement because they do not fit the actual processes and tools employed by the organization. The numbering patterns they use imply a sequence that cannot be followed due to enterprise practices or organization dynamics. But these deficiencies can be overcome by adapting the methodology to the organization rather than trying to adapt the organization to the methodology. The successful implementation of a methodology generally requires forming a support group to provide coaching and to aid in definition.

Cost Models/Estimators

PRIMARY FUNCTION

These tools have two purposes: (1) to establish the budget for the project and (2) to provide a target for individual work efforts. The typical cost model/estimator provides estimates of the effort (days or hours), cost (based on average workday calculations), and duration required.

YEAR 2000 RELEVANCE

The coming of the millennium has not significantly altered the makeup of these tools. If you find one that meets your requirements, employ it. Most organizations do not have such tools, instead relying on intuitive estimates provided by experienced support personnel. Estimates of this nature can be relatively accurate, but demand a detailed evaluation of requirements. More often they are off by as much as 200 percent due to unforseen problems and overconfidence.

IDIOSYNCRASIES

The better cost models/estimators have the ability to enter the incidence of date-related definition and processing lines to be modified and redesigned. The tool accepts input on such important factors as employee knowledge of the application, complexity of the application, documentation requirements, availability of computing resources, schedule and risk constraints, tools usage, data complexity, and management.

One caution—and it's a significant one—with these tools: The tools can be manipulated to produce an "expected" forecast; that is, to produce false information. So if yours is an organization in which accurate information is welcomed only if it has positive implications, using these tools can result in an underestimation of the costs for the update project, in effect rendering the implementation of these tools useless. Be honest with yourself and your enterprise, and remember, sometimes the truth hurts.

A final note: As you begin to generate estimates, set up a process whereby the actual results are documented against the estimate. Firms that use function points will be familiar with benchmarking, which means that regardless of the estimating tool used, such organizations have characteristics that skew the actual performance. Thus the tool should allow for applying benchmark results back into the model.

STAFFING IMPACT

Cost modeling and estimating is best left to a few trained staff. One or two people trained in the use of this kind of tool should be sufficient to support a large enterprise.

Relationship Mappers

PRIMARY FUNCTION

This tool looks at job-scheduling instructions to determine which programs are run together in a job. It can also tell you where data files are created and used, which programs use them, and which files are passed across system and application boundaries.

YEAR 2000 RELEVANCE

A relationship mapper establishes knowledge about the passing of data within and between applications. This information is required to plan the building of bridge files and to determine the need for concurrent changes or to set precedence of changes. Such knowledge reduces delays in implementation and can help to prevent constructing unnecessary bridges and performing extra testing.

IDIOSYNCRASIES

A typical commercial relationship mapper does not provide a detailed enough analysis to reveal all components involved in an update project. Its use of job-scheduling instructions automatically eliminates all programs that are performed or executed in real time—driven by transaction events or hardware "interrupts." These do not show up in the schedules. They are invoked by the computer when an event is detected by a routine that is constantly running. The problem with this tool, as mentioned in Chapter 1, is that it does not take an "enterprise view." It is confined to looking at the processes performed on one platform and generates data in the form of charts and diagrams. These are not all that useful until the knowledge they represent is moved into a data store that provides the complete enterprise context—a repository (discussed later). And be aware that nearly all of the commercial tools of this type are limited to IBM mainframe processors.

STAFFING IMPACT

Running a relationship mapper does not require much technical skill, and it can be learned in a few hours. However, extracting useful information from the run does require an analyst familiar with the application being mapped. Data entry support usually is provided by staff who run the tool, since they are familiar with the output. In addition, because information from multiple applications is being captured at one time, it is necessary to provide supervision and coordination to several analysts. Finally, keeping the resulting knowledge base up-to-date requires the implementation of change control.

Repository

PRIMARY FUNCTION

In computer parlance, a *repository* is a collection of information about a computing system, including the relationship of the elements of information to one another. The industry has attempted to define exactly what information should be included in a repository and how one should be constructed. Alas, there is still no standard, and therefore many different vendors use the term "repository" to refer to their own special files in which they store "things" that are important only to those using their products.

YEAR 2000 RELEVANCE

The purpose of the repository in the update project is to track all the knowledge required to manage the work and resources of the organization. Unfortunately, Year 2000 repository requirements are much broader than those served by the best-known repository providers; they must include all the information required to plan and track progress toward fixing the problem. A Year 2000 repository will track business functions, organizations, applications, subsystems, projects, computer "jobs," code components, data components, platforms, hardware components, system software components, embedded systems, forms, reports, screens, test data, and scripts. This information then can become your checklist of what has been changed and what still needs to be changed.

Repository products include a data collection component, a data retrieval component, and a report writer. Interfaces enable the capture of status information. Some repositories link to library and configuration management tools and produce project plans and schedules. Others keep track of estimates and record the duration and effort performed. Certain of these tools are sold with optional interfaces; or you may elect to construct additional ones.

IDIOSYNCRASIES

The most important capability of the repository is the building and maintenance of relationship information. All the elements in the repository are related to multiple components. Thus a repository that limits the number and type of relationships will not provide the information required to manage the update, because it is the relationship information in the repository that tells you, for example, the impact of a late vendor delivery on project work schedules, data, other applications, and business functions. Through the chain of relationships it is possible to show how the failure to replace a PC can cause the interruption of a product line. This knowledge can't be obtained in any other way. Unfortunately, most available repositories are limited in scope to the application code components and do not capture or support any other information.

An ideal product will also list specific lines to be changed or modified, reveal opportunities for setting standards; indicate the location of date routines; identify effort required at component level, and show where bridges need to be constructed.

STAFFING IMPACT

Staffing requirements vary according to the complexity and scope of the repository in use. Implementing a repository may require significant changes to computing management processes; and adaptation of any existent process definitions follow from that change. Support staff is required to manage the data and ensure it is current. Since much of the information required (i.e., information about hardware and systems software, embedded systems, suppliers and vendors, and so on) is not stored on a computer, be prepared to conduct significant research and data entry during the load process. Consequently, there will be ongoing clerical requirements for managing and editing the data.

Project Planning/Tracking

PRIMARY FUNCTION

Project planning/tracking tools perform the functions of scheduling tasks, defining precedence and dependencies and allocating tasks by resource. Some of the oldest and most advanced tools support the functions of project planning and tracking. More than 100 project planning and tracking tools are available to assist managers with resource load leveling and to identify hidden staffing and hardware resource requirements. Tracking capabilities enumerate completed tasks, problems with estimates and skill requirements, and deviations from plan.

YEAR 2000 RELEVANCE

The more complex and time-critical the millennium update project, the greater the need for project management tools to enable communication of status information and manage the resources assigned to the project. Studies have shown that projects that are not carefully managed and do not receive management attention are 300 times more likely to fail. Remember, the Year 2000 project is a large and complicated one involving the updating of millions of lines of code and changing of components that do not include code. There is no way to track the progress of such tasks without the use of such a tool.

IDIOSYNCRASIES

Most planning tools are not sophisticated enough to provide a single complete plan for the date problem. There are just too many tasks. Many enterprises overcome the limitations by dividing the project into smaller ones to plan at different levels of detail. This enables them to use the features of the simpler, but more intuitive, planning and tracking tools that run on PCs. The more complex the functionality of the planning tool, the better it becomes at supporting large project schedules, but the more difficult it is to learn.

STAFFING IMPACT

These products are generally used by centralized project managers, although the technical staff may maintain the plan at lower levels of

detail. Build in a three- to five-day training cycle for this type of tool.
You may want to delegate task completion and time-tracking data entry
to an administrative person. Some enterprises do not use the tool's
time-tracking capability, but enter status changes only in the repository.
Many tracking tools are interfaced with proprietary time-keeping/
reporting and billing products. These are often built by the computing
organization and serve the reporting needs of the enterprise.

Workflow Managers

PRIMARY FUNCTION

Workflow managers come in several varieties. The lowest-level tool
simply provides diagramming techniques for describing workflow
processes and interorganization interfaces. Higher-level tools include
e-mail connectivity to keep staff informed of activities and move
work along.

YEAR 2000 RELEVANCE

The advantage of having a workflow manager is that it simplifies communications in large, complex projects where numerous people are
involved, and moving work from one station to another is time-critical.
This tool can shave days, even weeks, off the cycle time of important
tasks. Managers will find that the tool will reduce the need for meetings and give them greater freedom once they get use to the process.

IDIOSYNCRASIES

The networking requirements to introduce the more advanced tools
are significant, but worthwhile. The chief concern in implementing a

workflow manager is just getting everyone to use it—if anyone fails to employ the tool properly, it will cause the tool to fail entirely. Usually, getting people to communicate is the cause of a bottleneck, and often, management resists the tool more than does technical staff, because they are more comfortable with verbal than with written communications.

STAFFING IMPACT

To launch a workflow manager successfully generally requires two months of training and coaching. But staffing support requirements are minimal once the launch is complete. A local area communications network is required; therefore an administrative person needs to manage the message files and access security. This is often handled by the network administrator.

Library Managers

PRIMARY FUNCTION

Many organizations have used code libraries for a long time. These tools store code and keep track of different versions. They allow the user to attach code modules, and are used by some to track code and test data components. Features of some products help to locate missing components and facilitate identification of obsolete components. Reusable code can be saved as code modules and "copied" into or "included" in other programs. Many library managers include a "checkout" process that allows people to get a copy to look at or work on. Conversely, a "check-in" process allows the system to track changes so that multiple versions of the code can be stored.

YEAR 2000 RELEVANCE

Year 2000 relevance of library managers stems from the need to provide specific storage locations for all code. Computer people are notorious for keeping code components in private files, team files, and application files, making them difficult to find and manage. Bringing this code under control is part of the inventory process. A library manager provides a minimal amount of control over those components.

IDIOSYNCRASIES

A number of library managers have been implemented on more than one platform, which may prove relevant in a multiplatform environment because common user interfaces cut training time. Many hardware vendors include library management tools with the systems software that is purchased with the hardware.

However, standards must be created and enforced. Use of the library manager must be universal or the process will break down quickly as new code components are purchased or created. One reason that library management tools fail to be implemented is the absence of naming conventions or control of naming standards. Enterprises that purchase many applications from outside cannot control vendor names, causing conflicts with names and naming conventions.

STAFFING IMPACT

If the enterprise has—and enforces—naming conventions, library management tools are relatively easy to implement and require relatively little support and maintenance. On the other hand, an enterprise could find itself faced with months of activity if it must create and implement naming standards. In such situations, the organization may simply not have the time or resources to employ such a tool.

Change/Problem Managers

PRIMARY FUNCTION

Change/problem managers track implementation schedules and projects for operations team. They are used to coordinate changes with the staffs in programming, technical support, database administration, and operations scheduling.

YEAR 2000 RELEVANCE

The Year 2000 project benefits most from these tools during the migration stage, though they are also helpful for tracking parallel changes. Coordinating the implementation schedule is simplified by the existence of this type of tool.

IDIOSYNCRASIES

The implementation of the change management function is not always easy. Most enterprises already have some form of manual change management process in place. For those enterprises, the greatest difficulty will be to find the tool that supports the process already employed. Changing an existing process to fit the tool will create frustration. Consequently, communication failures resulting from the new process will be viewed as a failure of the tool and lead to its abandonment.

STAFFING IMPACT

Process definition and documentation can require several weeks of effort. Training is very client-specific and includes training in the process and the tool. Analyst and programmer training may require one to two days. The change management process needs to be reflected in the factory process and should be included in project plans as milestones. The tool itself rarely requires support or maintenance.

Configuration Managers

PRIMARY FUNCTION

Configuration managers align source code and machine language versions during the development and maintenance cycles so that the wrong version is not placed in production or lost. They provide excellent information on the relationships of components to other components, job streams, and applications. The tool includes security definitions that limit access to the person who is in the process of changing the code. The configuration manager also keeps track of code-component relationships so that any code checked out for change automatically checks out components. Other staff members can look at the code and even obtain copies, but they cannot release a copy back into the environment except through the individual who has checked out the code. Most configuration managers support one or more interim libraries where the code is retained in various status levels (e.g., work, test, migration, production). Movement of the code from one status to another requires special authorizations. This is necessary so that groups of components can be staged for testing or movement to production.

YEAR 2000 RELEVANCE

Next to methodology, configuration managers are probably the most important tools employed in the Year 2000 project. The payoff comes from validating that all code in a change group is simultaneously moved through the change process and implemented. This payoff includes making sure that code for conversion programs and bridge programs are implemented at the same time.

IDIOSYNCRASIES

Configuration management tools are among the most difficult to implement because they require significant organizational work up front. The reason is that all ongoing work must be transferred to the tool, and no shop has all its applications static at a given point in time. The complexity of the start-up is made apparent by the definition of the processes the tool performs. These processes are most often used in concert with change management and library management tools.

Some versions of this type of tool run in several environments—computer platforms and operating systems. Organizations with mixed environments may find that this significantly cuts learning and implementation cycle times.

STAFFING IMPACT

We do not recommend implementing this tool as part of the Year 2000 correction program if it has not already been started, because preparation can be very resource-demanding. Administration requirements are different among the tools. Some may require only a part-time administrator, while others may require several full-time administrators. If, however, you have a configuration manager in place, it will pay for itself many times over.

Distribution Managers

PRIMARY FUNCTION

Distribution management tools are used to schedule and perform the downloading of software from one site to many. Many enterprises have already found it necessary to provide a mechanism for tracking multiple copies of software. Distribution managers were originally developed for use in distributing internally developed mainframe/midsize application software to multiple sites.

Increases in the practice of central distribution of PC software has resulted in the creation of a form of this tool that keeps track of the version of every software program loaded on servers and clients. This often becomes necessary to prevent violating product licensing agreements. These surrogate managers schedule transfer of software versions to individual computers through network resources. The status of each software program version on every target platform is maintained in a file so that the status of the product's distribution is known.

YEAR 2000 RELEVANCE

According to a Microsoft Internet recommendation, the Year 2000 resolution will require all PC software to be replaced when the ball drops in 1998.

Implementing this tool will help users compile the existing PC software inventory and support the expense of replacing hardware and software. Although the tool is designed to work within a network, some organizations have found its inventory capabilities valuable enough to implement *before* they establish the network. Without this tool, the distribution of PC software can be haphazard. Some remote computers may continue to run old versions of software that

can fail, possibly propagating bad data back into the IT environment
and thereby damaging enterprisewide services as fast as they can be
corrected to support Year 2000 processing.

IDIOSYNCRASIES

Doing the PC and components inventory may take several months,
but programs are available to perform this task. Enterprises often discover that they cannot substantiate legitimate licenses, because copies
of some licenses exist on many machines. This is often the result of
grabbing the first copy that can be found to reload a PC. Therefore,
such enterprises may find it necessary to develop additional management processes. Implementing this tool can be done parallel to the
update process.

STAFFING IMPACT

Building an organization to manage distribution is often required. It
may take months to achieve but the payback justifies the expense.
Distribution management software requires administration support.
This product is typically run by a small staff of people who support
networks and parallel mainframe environments. Training runs from
two days to a week.

Version Managers

PRIMARY FUNCTION

Version managers make it possible to carry out concurrent change
projects and implement multiple changes to the same programs

because they provide the capability for simultaneous changes to be merged. Where the tool finds the same lines changed, conflicts are highlighted so that they can be reviewed; the changes can then be combined manually. When version managers are used, then, interim versions can be placed in production, tested individually, or held for a single release.

YEAR 2000 RELEVANCE

Many organizations cannot freeze application functions long enough to make the changes necessary for Year 2000 compliance. They may be forced by competition, regulatory requirements, environment changes, or Year 2000 failures to introduce several changes while code redesign to fix the Year 2000 problem is under way.

IDIOSYNCRASIES

This tool is important and easy to implement. Many variations provide adequate information to show differences between the original state and the changed state of the code product, potentially making it unnecessary to acquire a separate comparator tool (described later). Unfortunately, version managers are not available for most hardware platforms.

STAFFING IMPACT

Version managers do not require much training. Skill requirements for running the tool are minimal. A couple of hours' training is usually sufficient to enable a programmer to use the tool.

Analysis Tools: Scanners and Parsers

PRIMARY FUNCTION

Scanners and parsers examine individual computer code modules. Scanners are the simpler versions of the two; they search for matches of character strings in source code, but do not distinguish between data definition and process occurrences, and often do not distinguish between real code and comments. Parsers are a little more intelligent. They recognize the structure of the language and can distinguish not only where a date element is found, but also how it is used. Parsers can be used to trace date movement and find aliases that might not be found by a scanner.

YEAR 2000 RELEVANCE

Scanners and parsers are put to use twice during the Year 2000 correction process: first to estimate the number of lines with date occurrences and second, in the analysis process, to identify every date occurrence and flag the lines for further study and/or change.

Scanners are usually employed in the estimating process because they are faster and, when creating estimates, accuracy is not so important. Parsers are used primarily during analysis. These tools are easy to construct, and commercial products are also available that provide the ability to find date fields using many different combinations of date field name formats. Users will also find it handy to be able to exclude some character strings that would otherwise create false matches (e.g., that don't interpret DD in the work ADD as a date reference).

IDIOSYNCRASIES

Many scanners and parsers have been tailored to support the Year 2000 update process, but they usually support only COBOL. Many specially designed products do not give the purchaser much freedom in defining the search arguments, and the list provided may prove inadequate. This limitation may be a handicap where the application employs naming conventions that are not easily identified as dates (e.g., ADVYRAHEAD, used to specify a table item containing the next year, in which YR is buried in the field name, making it hard to find). It can be a real showstopper when foreign languages have been employed to define data fields.

If you decide to purchase a commercial scanner or parser, look for the ability to exclude terms, because many employ naming conventions using abbreviations such as DA (confusing DATA with DAY) or MO (confusing MOVE with MONTH) to be identified as dates. The exclusion capability allows the user to exclude words or to look for patterns at the beginning of a variable name, possibly followed by a special character such as a dash, and exclude them.

STAFFING IMPACT

These tools are relatively easy to use and do not require much training. Several are available for mainframe use, and they exist for most platforms. The best ones run on PCs, but this usually means that the program code has to download, a time-consuming process for large volumes of code.

Data Modeling and Design Recovery Aids

PRIMARY FUNCTION

These tools have been developed over the last few years to support product reengineering. While some of early data modeling tools required manual development of diagrams to show the flow, newer products perform the work of decomposing the code into functional blocks or "slices." The flow diagrams are generated automatically to show both data and control flow from slice to slice. These diagrams define business rules.

The segmentation of the code is useful for building "objects" or discrete functions, which can then be reused. However, the output of these products is not standard. Some will provide new versions of the code that are restructured and cleaned of unused code. Others will produce process flow and data flow diagrams; still others provide quality metrics.

YEAR 2000 RELEVANCE

Data modeling and design recovery aids can prove beneficial during the millennium update project in three ways. Enterprises faced with the possibility of abandoning proprietary code may find these tools essential for analyzing the functions so that they can assess the loss and conduct salvage operations or create specifications for vendor packages. They can supply the documentation needed to redesign programs that are difficult to read and unsupported by experienced staff. They can also assist in defining reusable components such as date routines and conversion programs.

These tools are also useful in populating and automatically maintaining the relationships between code and function in a repository.

IDIOSYNCRASIES

These tools take many forms, but most exist for use on PC-based workstations. They can be beneficial in building models and documenting the process to provide cycle-time reduction improvements during the Year 2000 project. They can aid in assessing product quality, determine the functional paths that need to be included in test script development, and eliminate unused or redundant code that does not require changing. But be aware that these products are computer language–specific, although a number of them can handle more than one language.

STAFFING IMPACT

The operator of this tool is generally not your average programmer; it requires experience and technical decision making. Training time is roughly three to five days, and the learning curve is from two to four months.

Documentation Aids

PRIMARY FUNCTION

A documentation aid is similar to a reengineering tool, but operates at a slightly higher level. Many provide analysis of job run instructions, creating job flows that show program and data file usage and highlight files that are imported from outside the enterprise or the application. Many provide useful cross-reference listings for compiling aggregate information at the application level.

YEAR 2000 RELEVANCE

Documentation aids are of greater benefit to enterprises that do not have a repository. They can provide much necessary information about relationships of code and data that will help prevent costly mistakes caused when code or data used by other applications is changed without making changes to the other applications. It is not a replacement for the repository, which is a more globally useful tool.

IDIOSYNCRASIES

Documentation aids comprise a broad category of tools ranging from the very simple to complex. Most enterprises acquire several documentation aids. Some show the relationships of date fields across programs and data files, and they have been used for data administration and building data warehouses, as well as providing data flow diagrams for reengineering projects. These tools provide input to the repository.

STAFFING IMPACT

Documentation tools are used most often by analysts. The time required to learn these tools is dependent on the complexity of the tool. If detailed processes and run instructions are defined and constructed by the computer professionals, these tools can be operated by nontechnical staff. Most organizations that purchase these tools create programs to take the data generated and load it into databases or a repository.

Change Tools: Editors

PRIMARY FUNCTION

The features included with editors can significantly reduce the workload of the programmer. With many editors you can perform the following functions: scroll through components based on flow and paragraph execution; view included members on-line; locate field cross-references; uncover hidden date components; shorten data entry by providing statement constructs and basic syntax; identify similar modules for creating common routines; make global changes of words or phrases as in word processors.

YEAR 2000 RELEVANCE

Program changes are made using an editor. A good programmer with a good editor can process code changes as fast as another can using an intelligent editor (discussed next). Using an editor has the further advantage that it can be used for all work, as it is not restricted only to Year 2000 changes.

IDIOSYNCRASIES

Most computer people already use editors that were provided by the vendor with the hardware platform. The purchase of editors is, therefore, seldom even a topic, although many enterprises have purchased commercial editors in conjunction with programming workstations.

A good editor should have the ability to trace the flow of data through the process from one data element to the next, and provide tagging of the lines involved so that when changes are made, they can be captured and fed back to a central store. Many editors provide hot keys, which save the time it takes to type common words and computer commands.

STAFFING IMPACT

Most editors require only a day of training, usually provided by the vendor; but to become proficient may take several weeks. Even though most editors have similar functions, the introduction of a new one often meets with resistance, and thus is best done by a small group of proponents who can encourage the rest of the staff to adopt the new tool.

Rule-Based Change Tools: Intelligent Editors

PRIMARY FUNCTION

Intelligent rule-based editors rely on the ability of a human being to provide the definition of what a date is and is not. (For example, when does YR represent "year" and when is it used as a phonetic abbreviation for "wire"? No kidding, it happens!) The rules for making the changes are selected from a set provided by the vendor and constructed in the sequence to fit the situation (e.g., rule 1 might be to reformat dates from MMDDYY to YYMMDD; rule 2 might be to expand years from two digits to four digits when in character strings or to two three-digit forms when in packed decimal). The rules have to be validated manually; thus they require careful definition and, sometimes, customization. The first part of the rule application process is to identify the need to change the code. The second part is to replace the old code with new code.

These tools change more than one segment of the code (e.g., data definitions, procedure definitions, called subroutines, shared copybooks) during a single pass. Most intelligent editors annotate the changes made, provide helpful hints, and alert the operator to potential problems. These tools usually support a variety of data management software products and communications products for a single platform. As by-products of the process, the intelligent editor can provide information on test path requirements and create program templates that can be used to develop test program data, bridge programs, or conversion programs.

YEAR 2000 RELEVANCE

We use the label "intelligent editor" to describe the myriad tools and services that are appearing on the market purporting to "solve the Year 2000 problem." The most basic tool of this ilk automatically detects and expands the data definition of Gregorian and ordinal/Julian date fields containing years in two-digit format. This is not as simple as it sounds, however, because the product must handle a variety of date formats and storage techniques.

The most intelligent of these editors perform a variety of date change functions. They perform process instruction changes for all dates, including fiscal and period dates; they handle mixed dates, where some contain two-digit-year designators and others four; they automatically examine sizes of fields so that screen displays and reports won't exceed parameters; they track movement of dates to new fields (even when field names do not readily identify themselves as date fields) to make sure those fields will accommodate the new size.

IDIOSYNCRASIES

These tools are available on a variety of platforms. While most run on the PC, some are now being sold to run on IBM mainframes. The dominant focus of these tools is COBOL code, since it is the single most commonly used programming language. Many more tools supporting other languages are appearing—for example, assembler, PL/I, Natural, and Easytrieve. Expect many more of these tools to become available in the near future.

Rules are always developed at some central location by the vendor, and the process can become complicated. As the number of rules increases, the length of time to define a new one also increases. A quick analysis of date validation routines uncovered more than 30 different methods for performing the validation. Some require partial code replacement and others full replacement. Some programs use more than one routine, and the use of different formats may require the alteration of several validations.

Depending on how the rule is constructed and the sequence in which the rules are applied can result in errors being inserted. For example, the first action might be to insert a window. The first test might be to confirm whether the year is 00, then reject it as incomplete data. The test might never be satisfied because the year is now always 2000. You might want to remove the test or replace the initialization routine that loads the data entry mask with the null values instead of 0s. The year-validity test may require the value YY to be greater than 50 and less than 99, 01 to 97, greater than or equal to the current year, less than the current ear, within *n* years of the current year, and so on, in which case you might want to replace the acceptable range of YY or change the calculation that sets the value of the ranges. If 99 was once used to denote something other than 1999 (e.g., an indefinite date) but is now needed to denote 1999 quite specifically, you might have to change the process that inserts 9s in the date and every place it looks for 9s. Do not be surprised to hear quotes of up to two weeks to create one or more rules.

The best process for using intelligent editors is to first perform a design review using a parser. Find processes that are not covered by the rules (e.g., replacing calls to the retrieve the system date with calls to retrieve a proprietary date), then ask the vendor to add a rule to cover those processes you expect to recur. At the same time, you can make the change manually and proceed with the process so as not to hold up work, thus improving workflow.

Contrary to some marketing claims, intelligent editors are not silver bullets. A typical tool requires the operator to specify date definitions that "seed" a parser for what to look for to identify dates. The operator may need to make several passes to determine all the seeds and eliminate invalid identifiers. Further, these tools have a limited set of rules, so many of them fail miserably when tested against even simple examples. In one documented test, one of these intelligent editors found only 15 percent, 0 percent, and 25 percent, respectively, of the date changes required in three programs. Worse, it changed fields that should have been left alone.

STAFFING IMPACT

Intelligent editors can be bought with or without services. The service providers generally run the code and find the requirements for creating new rules. Where a service is used, plan on human support for it—someone who is intimate with both the rules used by the tool and the application being changed. Maintaining knowledge of the rules may prove difficult if the work is performed in a vendor factory. Multiple clients may be constantly generating rule requirements, rendering it virtually impossible to know the rules in place at any moment.

Installing and sustaining an intelligent editor can be difficult, especially if you take on rule definition, although running the tool is simple enough for a relatively nontechnical worker to perform.

Date (Clock) Simulators

PRIMARY FUNCTION

Date simulators intercept program calls to the hardware or system clocks. They are used to force the application to act as if it were running in another time.

YEAR 2000 RELEVANCE

This type of tool is critical for testing applications that have been changed to be millennium-compliant. It allows the user to tell the program that it is running in the year 2000, on February 29, 2000 or another date such as December 31, 1999. Without this tool, testing on some platforms cannot be completed.

IDIOSYNCRASIES

Date simulators began to appear in 1993 and have evolved significantly since then. Nevertheless, many organizations still encounter problems when using these tools to test in environments where concurrent changes are being made, because the test files get corrupted. Alternatives to using this tool include elimination of calls to the system clock and using a client-controlled clock. Some enterprises have found it more efficient to purchase another processor, or to lease time at a service provider that supports Year 2000 testing, to change the system clock to the date required.

STAFFING IMPACT

This is another tool that is easy to teach to a programmer, usually taking less than a day. It does, however, require constant administration to schedule its use and manage the date settings so they do not conflict with other tests.

Code (Static) Analyzers

PRIMARY FUNCTION

A static analyzer is a programming language–specific tool that audits programs to determine whether they follow the language rules. Violations of syntax rules are highlighted, making this an excellent precompiler diagnostic, hence saving cycle time on the target test computer.

Most static analyzers also allow specification of client-specific rules so that infractions can be identified. Nearly every one of these tools performs a quality assessment of the code to reveal introduction of new complexity that makes the program even more difficult to maintain.

YEAR 2000 RELEVANCE

In a situation where programmers are unfamiliar with the language of the program being changed, this type of tool provides an important teaching function. As resources become more difficult to allocate, the presence of this tool enables less-skilled staff to be introduced to code change and testing process tasks.

IDIOSYNCRASIES

Very few languages are supported by code analyzers.

STAFFING IMPACT

Using code analyzers is rather straightforward, but building a special rule set may take several weeks and the assistance of a programmer. Goals need to be determined and communicated to the staff, and auditing the use of the tool is required.

Interactive Debuggers

PRIMARY FUNCTION

A debugging tool allows the programmer to observe a running program to determine where it is failing and what data or situation is causing the failure. This tool reduces the amount of time required to solve problems.

YEAR 2000 RELEVANCE

While useful in testing programs that have been redesigned to achieve millennium compliance, the chief benefit of a debugger will be in identifying failures in production that occur due to date failures.

IDIOSYNCRASIES

Debuggers are available for a number of computer languages, and many run on PCs or have a much friendlier PC front end. These tools can be impressive when used in testing changes. It is possible to use these tools to temporarily alter the date values at specific points in the program and then watch the value as it is passed through the program. You can actually see the changes that take place and identify the lines of code that are not performing the change as expected. You can even fix the code and restart the process at that point. This may obviate the use of a date simulation tool for some testing.

STAFFING IMPACT

These tools take several days to learn—and weeks for the programmer to become proficient. They require significant programming experience to use, hence it may be prudent to have only the most knowledgeable programmers use them in diagnosing production problems.

Code Comparators

PRIMARY FUNCTION

This product performs a line-by-line comparison of two versions of a program or file. When a mismatch is identified, the two lines are reported either on-line, for interactive evaluation, or in a printed report.

This tool is used in two ways. The first and most frequent is to confirm that changes in reports or files have been made as expected. The second is to determine what has been changed in the source code. The latter is usually done when the code is changed by some-one who does not work for the enterprise—the purpose being to check for unauthorized alterations.

YEAR 2000 RELEVANCE

Comparators can reduce testing cycle time and validate not only the tests, but the changing of test data. If code is sent out to a ven-dor factory, a comparator can rapidly validate the changes made in the factory, and it may be possible to skip some global testing of all routines since it is easy to determine the altered lines that require testing.

IDIOSYNCRASIES

There are few of these tools, but they are easy to build, so most enterprises have constructed their own. They do not have to be language-specific, though some find it useful to build in exclusionary rules for things like line numbers or changes in comments.

STAFFING IMPACT

Since they are easy to run, comparators can be almost fully automated. The actual review of the output, however, will require an experienced computing professional familiar with the programming language or data.

Code Generators/4GLs

PRIMARY FUNCTION

There are several forms of code generators. Their purpose is to reduce the time it takes to create a program. Code generators make it simple to create the programs that extract data for testing, to make changes to data for testing, to generate data-conversion programs for inserting century values, and to build bridges.

YEAR 2000 RELEVANCE

This productivity aid will save time in creating conversion programs and bridges, building custom test data generators, or editing data. If you have to replace missing source code, code generators can save days of coding and testing. Some enterprises build special tools to replace date routines in the source code or to scan for dates.

IDIOSYNCRASIES

Some code generators are not themselves millennium-compliant, which obviously could cause problems in creating some specialized routines or making data changes. Some tools use preexisting data file definitions, while others require that they be reentered each time the file is used.

STAFFING IMPACT

These tools generally take some time to learn and become proficient with, but they can be taught to a noncomputer person. Many of them are similar to the report writers and macrolanguages used to create PC-based programs. An experienced PC person can become an expert with four to six weeks of constant practice. Programmers generally need more time to become proficient because they do not have the opportunity to use the tool constantly.

Test Scripters

PRIMARY FUNCTION

Testing is not an ad hoc process. It must be planned so that all the design changes are tested and all variations in the data are accounted for. The test-scripting tool facilitates the planning and documentation so that data can be created and the test run. This is required for several types of tests, including systems and acceptance testing. The playback feature enables the product to run the test. This is important for on-line application tests in which data is normally entered by an individual. The product acts in place of the person entering the data.

YEAR 2000 RELEVANCE

Test scripters enable the person who is changing the program to communicate with another regarding what changes to test and to what limits. In a factory environment where the testing agent and the person changing the code are different, this will save time and minimize the creation of test data.

IDIOSYNCRASIES

Certain test scripters are more difficult to learn and use than others, and most are written to support only on-line testing, so look for one that produces hard-copy scripts. Most platforms are supported by tools of this type.

STAFFING IMPACT

Scripters are usually used by experienced computer professionals, because their many functions can take weeks to assimilate

Date Routines

PRIMARY FUNCTION

Commercial date routines have the advantage of being fully tested. In enterprises that do not have standards, commercial date routines may provide an answer.

YEAR 2000 RELEVANCE

These routines are tested for millennium compliance. Replacing date processing with tested date routines may save time and reduce testing. When the rules for the date routine are built into a static analyzer, the programming of these routines can be delegated to less-experienced staff.

IDIOSYNCRASIES

If you are using workstations for making update changes, make sure the package supports testing on the workstation. Some are written in assembler for a specific platform. Choose a set that supports all the ways you store data. This requires some analysis, but it will save time later. Some enterprises store their data in several forms, including variations of size, edit masks, storage form (e.g., character, numeric, packed decimal, and binary), and even two-, three-, or four-digit-year fields.

STAFFING IMPACT

There is a limited set of code modules. Using them does not require specifically trained personnel, but identifying where and which routine to use may not be easy. Clients have employed over 100 routines for everything from date conversions to comparisons and arithmetic.

Migration Tools: Data Analyzers

PRIMARY FUNCTION

Many of these tools have been created to support the development of data warehouses and to help enterprise mergers. They perform an analysis of data files and look for patterns of data. They also find inconsistencies in data where patterns are known, such as nonnumeric date formats or variable date formats.

YEAR 2000 RELEVANCE

A data analyzer can identify hidden data, such as date data in fields that are not supposed to contain dates, or dates that are supposed to be invalid. In the Year 2000 update process, they can uncover hidden change requirements and be used to test the changes.

IDIOSYNCRASIES

Data analyzers are relatively new and thus may not be completely accurate or problem-free. Some require expertise that may not be available in-house.

STAFFING IMPACT

These tools require specialists. They should be run by a small staff who employ them frequently. Learning curves tend to be moderately high, with proficiency being reached in the third or fourth month of use.

File Definition/File Modification Aids

PRIMARY FUNCTION

These products are used to create file specifications for new files. They are platform-specific and create files for only a certain number of data management systems. They are, in essence, text editors used to define data files. They support allocating space, browsing existing data, editing data, and transferring data to new files.

YEAR 2000 RELEVANCE

This tool is used primarily to create test files. Where the data requires only the insertion of the century prefix 19, it can be used as a conversion program. Used in conjunction with a test-data generator, it will save time doing global editing of test data to simulate several dates.

IDIOSYNCRASIES

Certain of these tools provide a full set of functions, but on some platforms, the tools evolved with the functions split; hence, more than one tool may have to be purchased.

STAFFING IMPACT

File definition/file modification aids are used by computer professionals. Since they are powerful data editing tools, they are, in some instances, used instead of building a custom program to change production data, so the output must be tested. They require significant knowledge of the platform and the data management system being employed.

Test-Data Generators

PRIMARY FUNCTION

Test-data generators enable the user to define the rules for the data in a file and the limits of that data. The tool then creates a file with the data specified by the rules, which subsequently can be used in each phase of testing.

YEAR 2000 RELEVANCE

The typical mechanism used for creating test data is to select production data and then edit it by inserting and changing data as required to fit the test requirements. This process is inexact and time-consuming. This tool provides a far more accurate and complete set of test data without the additional work of editing.

IDIOSYNCRASIES

Before purchasing a data generator, make sure it is millennium-compliant. It must support dates generated across century boundaries. Some products do not support date definitions that include four-digit years. Although you can work around this deficiency, it is annoying and time wasting.

STAFFING IMPACT

These tools require one to two days of formal training or workshops. Like other data tools, knowledge of the system software and data management software is essential, which means that experienced computer professionals are required.

Database Conversion Tools

PRIMARY FUNCTION

Conversion tools are used by specialists to rebuild databases that have new formats. They are similar to file definition aids, but support data management systems.

YEAR 2000 RELEVANCE

These tools are used to expand field definitions and file sizes to allow for four-digit years.

IDIOSYNCRASIES

Most organizations already own these tools.

STAFFING IMPACT

These tools are used only by specialists trained in the management of databases built using data management systems. Again, this type of tool is one that requires some formal training, and it can take several months for personnel to achieve proficiency.

Chapter Ten

Won't You Please, Please Help Me

Even when an enterprise is ideally positioned, with the right staff and the management capability to handle the millennium update project, they still should probably ask: "Can we handle this ourselves?"

The general consensus among service providers is that *if* your enterprise is well staffed and well managed, *if* you've been given the necessary project resources, *and if* you started the Year 2000 correction process prior to 1995—that is, created a plan and a process, tested the process, and began changing code—then your enterprise can probably complete the change without help. Unfortunately, it's no longer 1995, and you *are* reading this book. That probably puts you in the company of about 99.5 percent of the enterprises in the world that are now in some degree of trouble.

In our opinion, probably no enterprise or organization will be able to solve this problem without some kind of help. Therefore, in this chapter we discuss why you might consider asking for help, what kinds of assistance you will find, where to look for that help, and what you can do to help the help help you.

Out of Source, Out of Mind

Few companies have both the capacity (time, people, facilities, and hardware) and the knowledge (understanding, experience, skill, and perception) required to perform all the work involved in the Year 2000 update project. Sadly, there are those that do not have either. Over the last 10 years, many enterprises have experienced massive downsizing. Further, some have implemented practices to restrict the growth of computer departments specifically. Among the casualties of restrictive measures are technical support staff, training programs, and training facilities.

In addition, techies in some organizations have been replaced with business-minded people, whose eyes are planted firmly on the bottom line and not code lines. Moreover, the educational system produces new graduates who are specialists only in the latest technical fads, while those skilled in computer languages, system software, and existing tools in many organizations have either retired or been forced out. These moves mean that many enterprises are ill-equipped to deal with the massive change demanded by the coming millennium.

Much has been written about outsourcing, and we recommend that you do a little (actually, as much as you can) investigation before you start working with service firms, especially if you don't have any prior experience. For starters, find a copy of the article "Strategic Sourcing: To Make or Not to Make," by Ravi Venkatesan, in the *Harvard Business Review* (Nov.–Dec. 1992, vol. 70, no. 6, p. 68). He listed five reasons why you should at least consider outsourcing. It is paraphrased here to more specifically apply to the Year 2000 problem resolution:

1. Improve process.
2. Sustain strategic focus.
3. Contain costs.

4. Improve management control.

5. Transfer knowledge.

IMPROVE PROCESS

In the first six months of the millennium update project, you will have to perform a number of unique tasks:

Conduct an enterprisewide tactical plan

Tool up

Build a testing environment

Manage vendor changes

Support suppliers

Change obsolete code

Reconstruct missing code

Manage enterprisewide changes

Capacity, by which we mean time, facilities, equipment, and staff, is going to be your first impediment. Time, of course, will always be of the essence, exemplified by enterprisewide planning.

Not planning is not an option. Those organizations that forgo it, thinking it is a waste of time, pay for it later—literally and figuratively. If planning is not conducted *for the duration of the project,* it can take 30 percent longer and require staffing levels that could be 50 percent higher than estimated. On the other hand, when planning takes too long, it becomes worthless because applications will start failing. By the way, six months is not too long. This doesn't mean you can't start changing code while you are planning. Many organizations start pilots as soon as they can identify the source code to work on.

Setting up the process involves selling the need, developing the process, changing the infrastructure to support its development, constructing it, and figuring out how to change the culture so that the plan actually is employed. Enterprises that never make it to the last step have bypassed one or more of the other steps. If you want your Year 2000 update project to be a success, you cannot bypass any of the steps.

Now that we've put the fear of time in your hearts, back to where to go for help—outsourcing. There are firms out there that have been through the process of enterprisewide planning for the Year 2000, and they can install that process and build a plan in the time required. You will find consulting firms that know what information is required about hardware, software, vendors, data suppliers, and embedded systems. They can provide the infrastructure support systems to support management of these functions.

Although you will probably still have to prepare detailed fallback plans for any of the project components not completed on time, you will find firms that can, within a couple of weeks, provide you with a descriptive analysis of how your business functions relate to your systems and how they are interdependent. And unless your enterprise maps the dependencies of business functions to applications, you will have to assign staff to study the relationships to determine how the business will be affected by the process decisions. Again, outside services with the right tools can do this faster and with better accuracy than most internal staff.

You may also have to perform a risk assessment to determine what the penalties will be—lost revenue, violations of laws or regulations, and impact on individuals and business relationships—but a consultant can provide awareness training and provide you with an objective process for conducting the assessment.

Another route that some enterprises take is to reduce the complexity of the environment by reducing the number of languages that have to be changed. Ernst & Young's Cleopatra product converts PL/I code to COBOL II. A single-language environment makes replacement of date routines easier, facilitates insertion of purchased and tested date routines, and encourages the use of more tools in the date change process. If you have a lot of assembler code, you may want to consider Software Migrations Limited's language migration tool, FermaT, that takes IBM Assembler and converts it to C, COBOL, and even other languages. Friedman and Associates provides a service to move code from one platform and/or database system to another. This is only a small sampling of the services you might access. Remember that some tools will come with technical support, but for others you will be required to contract for support.

SUSTAIN STRATEGIC FOCUS

Most enterprises that try to do it all themselves underestimate the complexity of the date problem, and soon discover they are unable to focus their energies to both solve the Year 2000 problem and continue to support business as usual. They find they have too few people with both the skills and the interest to perform the change work.

Chances are, you, too, are understaffed. Perhaps the people who built your applications are no longer with the company or are heavily engaged in new key development projects. If the latter is the case, these projects will have to be either put on the shelf or expedited to get them completed prior to the failure of a current application. In many cases, these development projects absorb the time of the most knowledgeable personnel.

Consulting firms can provide the help you need and supply project management talent with date problem resolution skill and experience. These companies, for the most part, provide training to their new hires in technology and tools, a task that you might not be able to support.

Focusing your enterprise's available resources on fixing the problem may not be possible. Most computer shops say they spend up to 70 percent of their resources on maintenance, but that is probably fudging the truth. Approximately 40 to 55 percent of the maintenance budget is spent in making functional modifications to existing applications. Between 20 and 30 percent of the maintenance effort is spent assimilating changes due to hardware or systems software upgrades. Making adjustments because of vendor software changes absorbs another 10 to 15 percent of the maintenance budget. The bottom line? Only 5 to 10 percent of the budget is currently spent in fixing code errors, which is the nemesis of the computing staff.

As systems start to fail due to date problems, the percentages will start to shift. As they do, less time will be available for the most experienced staff to spend on design problems or in managing the code change process. Since the hardware, systems, and vendor application software changes will increase, there will be additional pressure on resources dedicated to code changes. New development will be impacted by the increase in maintenance. Many of these projects will have to be completed on time because they are scheduled to replace applications that are not millennium-compliant.

Needless to say, during all this, competition will not remain idle. No enterprise can afford to lose ground against others in quality or performance. New functionality will be required even against competitors that are not making strides to become compliant. It will hardly serve your enterprise to lose sales as its expenses increase due to the cost of fixing the code.

CONTAIN COSTS

If you have a small company, containing costs may be problematic in subtle ways. You may have to find homes for additional staff. There may not be enough telephone lines or terminal ports. Large enterprises, too, will not be exempt from space constraints. One state government agency found itself looking for space to house 40 people for three years. Delays in doing so increased the agency's staffing requirement to 55.

Outsourcing the work to a company that provides its own facilities will save time and expenses. The tasks of finding the space and setting up furniture, telephones, and the like are all eliminated. And, because the duration of the need is finite, you will also save time and the expense of its ultimate divestiture.

Computer resources may also be obtained from the outside. A number of firms offer computers for disaster recovery and special development projects, and specifically for testing Year 2000 changes. These same firms may be the avenue of retreat if you do not have the storage capacity to handle both the testing and expansion of data fields.

IMPROVE MANAGEMENT CONTROL

A word to the wise: Project teams that were precipitous enough to begin working on the Year 2000 problem early have been stumped by an old foe: poor management control. These early-bird project teams have frequently found the cost of the changes and the duration of the individual correction projects consistently doubling. Why? Because IT organizations literally empty their drawers of every change request that had been put off for years for lack of a financial justification. Since they are now authorized to make changes that have no apparent financial return, Pandora's box has been opened

Going outside for labor support can keep the scope of work in check. External expenses require hard currency. Outside help will gladly make your changes, but they won't do it out of the goodness of their hearts, so management is more likely to curtail incremental project additions. This, then, releases the computer staff to pursue the day-to-day workload.

TRANSFER KNOWLEDGE

There are many service firms that can provide support in this regard, including but not limited to the following:

- Contract programmers and testers
- Consultants skilled in planning, project management, and testing
- Legal services that perform contract reviews
- Services that determine vendor status and track vendor progress
- Consultants who specialize in tool assessments and implementation
- Business consultants skilled in analyzing business risks
- Process reengineering specialists who can help design replacement applications
- Specialists in source code recovery
- Software factories that can update code in large quantities

Getting the attention of these service vendors is easy—sort of like waving a cape in front of a bull. Just be careful that you choose those that have experience in the issues related to the millennium update. The point of hiring help is not just to add a few extra hands and brains, but to expedite the accumulation of knowledge. There is little time for trial and error. We've said it before, and we'll say it again here: Very few companies are experienced in Year 2000 work. It takes about a year for a company to understand the problems associated with the intricacies of the Year 2000 fix, so be sure to verify references of any firm you are considering.

Taking Out a Contract

The easiest resources to find are contractors, but be sure you know what that means. Contract companies supply people; they do not always supply *skilled professionals*. Don't be surprised to see some programmers and analysts coming out of retirement to cash in on the Year 2000. These people will have all the experience and knowledge, but may require some time to refresh their memories if they have been out of the business for awhile. Watch out for people who are inadequately trained and without much technical experience. Care must be taken in the contract negotiations to clearly define the technical knowledge and skills required.

Contract people usually expect to be guided, directed, and managed by enterprise staff. They will require time to assimilate and be assimilated by your enterprise culture. They will require all the care and feeding of a new employee, including orientation and training in practices and procedures. A well-defined process will make this assimilation easier and faster. Contracted help can be introduced to the process piecemeal, with workload expanding as they become familiar with their requirements.

Before you decide to employ contractors, you may want to review which projects they are going to be working on. Some vendors do not allow contractors to work on their products unless they are licensed. Some systems may require special knowledge about the application. Banks, for instance, find contractors familiar with deposit systems are better when it comes to working on those systems. Some applications may be so sensitive that you will not want an outside person working on them at all.

I'm a Consultant

Hey, who isn't? You're going to be inundated with consulting-service providers that claim to have experience in massive conversions, language upgrades, and reengineering projects. They will point to proprietary processes that have been altered to deal with the Year 2000 problem. Trust no one; verify every claim; check every reference. Make sure your agreement is formal, complete, and explicit, not based on hype and poorly defined expectations. Remember, in contract disputes, service providers rarely find it difficult to prove customer complicity.

Planning Consultants

We don't mean to imply that reliable firms engaged in planning for Year 2000 since 1992 are not out there; they are, so look for them. Such a consulting company can complete the planning stage in about the same time your enterprise can get its staff together and create a project charter. Nonetheless, expect your involvement in the planning process to equal the consulting company's.

Not all planning proposals are the same, so evaluate the proposal submitted to you from a consultant on the basis of the company's experience, the breadth of the planning effort, the number of resources they are planning to assign, and the proposed duration.

Consulting companies that provide services like tools assessments and testing are not as easy to find. Many of these are aligned with selected tool vendors, so be sure you are aware of such alliances before they are hired. The true consulting firm will be able to provide an unbiased assessment of the tools you have and your ability to bring in others. Also verify that the firm assigns staff familiar with the platform for which the tool assessment is being performed.

Testing Consultants

There are consulting firms that specialize in testing, which are ideal candidates to test vendor products, as well as applications updated by an outside service group. These companies possess special testing tools, which can save your enterprise time and money that might be misspent in searching for tools and implementing the wrong ones. These firms do not need to be experienced in working specifically with the millennium update project. Most have already sufficiently studied the problem and understand the requirements.

Contract Service Consultants

There are also contract service companies that place an emphasis on supplying project teams. These companies have methods and experienced project management personnel who will be worth their weight in gold during the rush to meet the turning of the century clock. Unfortunately there are not many quality experts in this regard, so if you do hire such a firm, expect that it will start an experienced person on your project and then replace that individual with someone of lesser credentials. This is not a bad technique. The knowledgeable consultant will establish the process and train your people, then set up the knowledge transfer. The second string maintains and improves the process and manages the work.

Most full-service computer companies divide their offerings into a small number of categories:

Estimating the cost of the portfolio change activity
Helping to plan the code redesign
Providing resources to change the code

For the most part, these firms restrict their services to a single hardware platform and computer language.

Finding the consultant with the breadth of skills required for your enterprise will be a challenge. You may have to or choose to engage two or three different full-service firms if you can afford the time and can segment the work to eliminate finger-pointing in the event of problems.

Legal Consultants

Legal consultants do not require any special knowledge of the Year 2000 problem, although the legal community has done some investigation into the problems that may result beginning on January 1, 2000. Legal help thus can be engaged with little coaching and a minimum of preparation time. Use the legal summaries already on the Internet to provide the general direction. Web addresses do get old, but you might try these, as suggested by Jeff Jinnett of LeBooeuf, Lamb, Greene & MacRae:

- www.auditserve.com/yr2000/yrktrk.html
- www.itpolicy.gsa.gov/library/yr2000/y209rfpl.htm
- www.year2000.com/archive/warranty.html
- 204.222.128.9/horizon/year2000/drftspec.htm

Business Consultants

Finding business consultants and business process reengineers with the right kind of experience and focus will prove something of a challenge, because the methods used by most of these firms are designed for quality, not quick change processing. While specific Year 2000 experience is not a requirement for business consultants, these people should at the very least appreciate the urgency of the situation. The firms that will provide the most help are those specializing in rapid deployment of new systems.

Recovery Consultants

If source code recovery is required, you have only a few options. In fact, we know of only one in the United States (Source Code Recovery, Inc.), and this company offers a narrow band of services. It works only with code written for IBM mainframes and is limited in the number of languages it supports, namely, COBOL, Assembler, and PL/I. Plus, its services are very expensive, and the code you get back will not be pretty—nor will it include the Year 2000 changes. Still, having this code is better than no code at all. Expect to employ someone not only to make the Year 2000 fixes, but to maintain them as well.

Consultants via the Internet

Finding Year 2000 assistance has become easier thanks to the Internet. The Year 2000 Web site (www.year2000.com) lists numerous service providers. Subscribers can provide candid opinions of the services provided by these vendors. The Mitre Corporation (www.mitre.org/research/y2k/) provides an independent view of some Year 2000 tools. You can get a vendor's view of its offerings at www.year2000.com. If you are experienced in surfing the Internet, you can find ads from companies specializing in tools, services, and even consumer products such as mugs and T-shirts. (One search returned an advertisement for trenching tools; the advertisement was not computer disaster–related. Surfing the Net can provide you with a source of amusement when things get tough.)

Before You Buy

Before you hire an outside provider, be prepared for internal changes. Two practices employed by most enterprises probably will have to be abandoned when engaging outside help with your Year 2000 repair. The first is the *request for proposal* (RFP), and the second is the warranty on work performed. No, we aren't kidding. Let us explain.

RFP, Please

The RFP process not only takes a lot of time that you don't have, but requiring a response to RFPs also may eliminate your enterprise from consideration by the firms you send them to. We will be entering a period where the demand for resources will create a seller's market. Most RFPs are written without extensive knowledge of the requirements; they demand responses in a specific format and use up consultants' time creating those responses, which are primarily sales instruments.

Over the past few years, numerous discussions about the RFP process have been held on the Internet in the Year 2000 mail list. People have questioned what should and shouldn't be included in an RFP and even whether or not the RFP is useful in a situation where you might be forced to call in outside help and literally cannot afford the time to be choosy.

Here is a random selection of some of the more interesting requirements and queries we've seen proposed. These are reasonable requirements and serious questions. It cannot be denied that the answers will enable you to make a better buying decision. As you read them, put yourself in the vendor's shoes and consider what your honest reaction would be to the following.

Impact Analysis

We currently estimate that we have about 100 million lines of code (including comments and command language interfaces) comprising about 130 highly integrated applications. These are primarily COBOL (60 percent), and 10 percent is written in an in-house language called INSURE-X based upon an early version of APL, with the remaining code spanning about 15 additional languages in relatively equal proportions. They include C++, APL, SAS, BAL, BASIC, and Easytrieve.

Since our inventory is not yet complete, we estimate these figures to be within 50 percent of the final figures. We have not yet begun a comprehensive analysis of our data.

Given this scenario, we are looking for a service provider to take control of our Year 2000 project. Please provide as much detail as you can to the following questions:

1. Describe the methodology your organization uses to perform the Year 2000 impact analysis. This description must address our unique needs in that we are a multinational company operating in a decentralized control structure.
2. Which programming languages (including version numbers) do you support? What is needed to extend your support to other languages? Can your process support a situation where COBOL has been written by German programmers in German?
3. While our existing documentation is not complete, we see the Year 2000 problem as an opportunity to set strong docu-

mentation standards for the future. How will your analysis aid us in that objective?

4. We are already using a metadata repository (PRISM Directory Manager). Does your solution interface with that product? If not, which products do you support, and do you offer an option to extend support to other products?

5. Is your solution capable of documenting cross-platform interdependencies for both applications and relational databases? Our platforms include PC, client/server environments, and MVS mainframes.

6. We require your analysis tools to operate on PC and client/server platforms due to existing CPU constraints on our mainframe and miniplatforms.

7. In view of the sensitive nature of both our data and applications, we will require that all analysis be performed on-site. We will be happy to supply a fully secure area, since we will also require that we be in control of the security process.

8. Due to past mismanagement, we are missing slightly more than the industry average (3 percent) of source code. How does your analysis methodology handle missing source libraries for COBOL, SAS, and BAL?

II Conversion Services

Upon completion of the impact analysis we will have identified where, when, and to what degree our organization is at risk. The next step is to remove those risks through the process of code conversion. Please respond to the following queries regarding your code conversion services.

1. It is possible we will contract with one company for impact analysis and with another for conversion services. Are you willing to work with us under these conditions? (*Note:* This practice is not unusual with government contracts.)

2. Which languages (include version numbers) do you convert? What is needed to extend your conversion services to other languages? Again, please take into account COBOL programmed in German.

3. Our organization cannot support a "big bang" conversion strategy. This constraint makes it mandatory that all conversion strategies incorporate automatic creation of bridges and filters to accommodate data transfer from and to applications out of sync in the conversion process. Does your solution provide this service?

4. As in the analysis phase, our CPU constraints make it mandatory that the conversion process take place on the PC platform. Can you support this requirement?

5. Change-control and configuration-management strategies of your conversion must be described in detail before your proposal can be given serious consideration.

6. As in the analysis phase, our security requirements will necessitate that all conversions be performed on-site. We will supply a fully secure area, since we will also require that we be in control of the security process.

7. What other resources will you require us to supply during the conversion process? Please detail hardware, software, and people requirements.

III Testing

In the past our testing requirements have been stringent. We have, however, come to realize that a short time frame will force us to accept less than optimal testing using existing strategies. We are looking for a service provider that can overcome these difficulties and guarantee its work via the tesing process.

1. As in previous phases, all testing must be performed on-site. We will supply a fully secure area, since we will also require that we be in control of the security process.

2. Describe in detail your testing process, with particular focus on the resources you provide to assist in this process.

3. How are current dates tested on your system? Because of the integrated nature of our systems, we have installed features to keep all system dates synchronized. Will you require separate platforms for testing? Can you provide the hardware resources for these test environments?

4. Which parts of the testing process are you able to automate? How does that process work?

IV Training and Support

We recognize that in order to automate many of the tasks in the Year 2000 project, we must employ a significant number of new tools. Please describe how your company will assist us in acquiring the necessary skills to gain the required level of proficiency.

1. We estimate that our greatest need for external training and support will arise during the testing and implementation phases. What levels of support can you provide us at this time? Must we commit to these support levels at the beginning of the contract?

2. Assuming we wish to move ahead on training regardless of the assignment of this contract, please provide course outlines, schedules, and costs for all nonproprietary tools.

3. During all phases of the contract, will the resources you supply be provided by your permanent staff, or will they be subcontracted?

4. Assignment of this contract will be contingent upon the successful completion of a preliminary pilot project. Please provide the parameters of a pilot you would consider suitable for the proper demonstration of your solution. Naturally, we are eager to begin this pilot at the earliest possible date.

5. Please specify all resources—yours and ours—required for the initiation of this pilot project.

V Guaranties and Fixed-Price Options

The final and most important information we are seeking relates to your company's experience in this area and your ability to service us at optimal levels for the duration of the project.

1. Provide details of your experiences in large-scale system conversions over the past five years. Please indicate your turnover statistics for this same time period so we can estimate how much experience has been retained in your organization.

2. How many customers are currently under contract, and when do these contracts expire? We need this information to ascertain that you will be able to deliver the proper level of support during all phases of our project; it will be too late if we discover in 1998 that you have staffing problems or conflicting service agreements.

3. How many past conversion were completed?

4. How many were delivered on time?

5. Please provide details on the size of these projects. Details should include a description of the change required and the number of lines, programs, applications, and databases changed.

6. Please provide cost estimates for all aspects of your proposal.

7. We are interested in fixed-price arrangements for all the proposed costs. What package deals are you prepared to offer us to secure this contract?

8. We require a guarantee of correctness for the Year 2000 conversion.

9. Please provide analysis of past proposal cost estimates compared to final completion and delivery costs.

10. Please provide references from past projects. These references need not be employed at the original company.

The preceding lists make many sensible and revealing points. Yet how quickly, when rolled up into an RFP, do reasonable questions start to seem like interrogation, with valid requirements becoming unrealistic expecations. Vendors have little inclination to respond to a barrage of questions when their doors are being beaten down by prospective clients wielding purchase orders.

We suggest you fully understand what it is that you are shopping for when you issue your request. Separate discussions of tool purchases from service purchases. If you are seeking services, decide whether you want consulting (planning and management) or contracting. If you want to contract the work, decide whether to do it inside, outside, or a combination. If the work is done inside, tell the vendor what the environment is (platforms, systems software, languages, data types, volume of programs); don't expect them to guess. Anticipate that people costs may escalate.

You, can, however, use a generic RFP, identifying the work to be done, volume of work, and length of time to generate a complete response. The computer service firms will also need to know when the work is to be performed on-site, what facilities and equipment are provided, and that the tools they are expected to use are in place. They will also ask what role your enterprise intends to play, so that they can determine their own. Don't get into discussions of ISO 9000. You are working on your own code, which was not built using ISO standards for documentation. Adding this requirement implies that you expect every bit of documentation to come out of the process. This adds to cost, and, when you may be fighting for survival, is meaningless. When it is important to document, pay for it.

Warranties and Pipe Dreams

We are always amazed at the enterprises that insist a consulting firm give a warranty on its work through the Year 2000. On the surface, it may not appear to be an unreasonable demand, but consulting firms will quickly explain that such a warranty is virtually impossible. First, a significant percentage of the changes are made at the discretion of the customer. The consultant can make recommendations, but the client provides the direction. The customer thus shares responsibility. Second, the consulting firm is dependent on the client's definition of "good data" and "bad data" for testing. The consulting firm tests only within the parameters provided by the client. Again, the client is sharing responsibility for the outcome. Third, the consulting company does not retain control over the code. Once the code is turned over to the client, any number of people can alter the code. This automatically voids any warranty.

FIXED-PRICE SERVICES

Be wary of offers of fixed-price services. Few services can really fix prices, and if they do, rest assured they will add caveats, rendering the fixed prices moot. Don't be taken in by this obvious sales mechanism to attract customers. Too many companies have already found out that such changes are rarely complete. Additional expenses are usually levied for repeat services and services not included in the contract. These expenses will be charged on the basis of time and materials. And fixed-price contracts will require tighter management than time-and-materials contracts.

Finding the Offer You Can't Refuse

There are several valid options for contracting out the code-fix work. Regarding the approach, you can choose manual, semiautomated, or fully automated. For the platform, you can choose to perform the change work on the target platform or move to PC workstations. As to location, you can choose to complete the changes on your computer, send the work to a domestic factory, or use an off-site factory.

APPROACHING THE RUNWAY

Let's clear up the approach terminology before you decide which way to go. For starters, the *manual approach* is not completely manual; it is computer-assisted, using scanners or parsers to locate date references and then using editing tools to make the changes. Testing for completeness employs a debugging tool to trace the logic. This process works for just about every computer language and on any platform.

The *semiautomated approach* employs a similar process. The process starts with the use of scanners and parsers to find the date field names. These are then fed to the change tool, which performs the process of expanding fields. The tool changes data definitions and logic to the best of its ability and generates programs to assist in century insertion and bridging. Note that the semiautomated approach will not make all your required changes. The change tool will either make incorrect changes or issue warnings that must be dealt with. A common example is expanding screen and report lines, exceeding the size allowed. These tools cannot replace human judgment and decision making.

The semiautomated approach is best for factories, because they can employ people at a lower cost due to lower skill requirements for some tasks, greater volumes of work uninterrupted by day-to-day problems, higher tools-use proficiency, and more experience in dealing with dates. This approach is currently available for COBOL, PL/I, NATURAL, FOCUS, Easytrieve, and RPG.

As of this writing, the *fully automated approach* is still just a twinkle in someone's eye; it has yet to be demonstrated. If it proves successful, it will eliminate the scanning and parsing steps. The code will be fed into the tool, and changed code will come out the other side. In addition, code will be provided for bridges so that no additional programming will be required. But the companies that are announcing they are close still require the customer to identify the dates, choose the rules, accept the result, and test the product themselves.

YOUR PLACE OR MINE?

The platform you choose is dependent upon the testing windows available. Some enterprises choose to do the work on computers already set up to support testing. These computers are populated with the tools owned by the enterprise and have such features as security and code management.

A second option is to purchase additional computers. IBM has recently developed a PC that runs mainframe software. These platforms can be populated with the same tools and changes, and testing can be performed behind a physical firewall. A bit of caution: The cost of installing tools on these units might be more expensive than they are worth.

Many enterprises have already moved to PC workstations, which are supported by an increasing array of tools that can be used to perform the changes. If your enterprise has started to move development and support to workstations, you will have the communications support installed and the procedures for doing the work remotely defined. If this is a new technology venture, hire help to get you started.

A third option is to lease time. Several firms offer disaster-recovery and time-sharing services to support Year 2000 fixes. These include security, tools, and management resources.

Regardless of what combination of options you select, be aware that you will need consulting company representatives on-site to organize the work, prepare it for transfer to the people changing the code, handle design questions with enterprise experts, receive the code, and participate in acceptance testing. Doing the work on-site may include setting up a factory environment. Some consulting services are now offering to bring the semiautomated approach on-site; the client is usually required to provide the equipment, communication facilities, and work services to support the factory.

Shipping the code off-site requires the establishment of communications between the host site and the work location. Factories are being set up in various sites around the world, in the United States, Canada, Ireland, and India. Other factories are in progress in the Dominican Republic, Singapore, the People's Republic of China, and elsewhere. These factories will need to address security issues—some applications cannot be shipped offshore for national security reasons. Another challenge will be time differences, which will impact voice communications and may require remote access during the busiest computer processing windows.

Obviously, an off-site solution reduces the demand on an enterprise's computer resources and facilities because the changes are made on the consultant firm's computer. Off-site firms may also be capable of limited testing, although the bulk of it will have to be conducted on the enterprise's host computer. Nevertheless, the enterprise is saved the cost of buying equipment, software tools, office furnishings, and support.

Finally, an off-site service provider may offer the advantage of one-stop shopping, because of its compatibility with diverse computer languages (such as Pacbase, FORTRAN, and C, in addition to COBOL) and its variety of hardware (including Hewlett-Packard, Digital Equipment, Sun Microsystems, or Unisys).

THE ACID TEST

If you decide to employ a consulting service, be aware that you will have to develop additional testing processes, because your consulting company will no doubt require that all your code be put through a baseline test before they accept the responsibility for changing it. Plus, your enterprise should establish an acceptance review process before allowing the code to be reinstalled on your computer.

The baseline test confirms that the code operates correctly in processing the current century dates. The baseline test recompiles the code to ensure that all components are available and that the version the code was written in can be compiled with the existing system software. The balance of the test determines whether the date routines handle standard processes correctly—comparisons, computations, searches, validations, including handling of leap years. Problems found during this test can be repaired either by the client or by the consulting firm—at additional expense, of course; and the consulting firm generally requires that it perform the test or that they be permitted to conduct a detailed review of the test performed by the client. Again, expect to pay for this activity, but do not begrudge the expense; it is not a ploy for getting more money. These tests almost always reveal problems with the existing code and data; thus they save time in making the changes and may eliminate some testing later.

The primary purpose of the review is to ascertain that all the components have been changed and are in the package and that the integrity of the application has not been compromised. The review also includes running a comparison of the baseline-tested code provided to the consultant and the code that has been changed. The review of the differences will uncover any failings in completeness or integrity. The review should also include a walk-through of any design changes that were required, any questions or issues identified by the people changing the code, and deviations from standard practices. Finally, the better consulting services will alert you to additional requirements for testing the code based on changes that were made.

Before You Sign on the Dotted Line

Before you execute the agreement to obtain services from another firm, be well prepared. Here are a few suggestions for your review; some of this is only common sense, but it never hurts to have a checklist to make sure nothing is overlooked.

1. Prepare a plan.

   - Identify exactly which products or data will be turned over to the service.

   - Enumerate exactly the results you expect when a product or data item is returned. If it is changes to the product or the data, define any constraints. If a new product is to be created, define each content item. Itemize security requirements and copy restrictions. If the service retains a copy, set limits to that retention.

   - Define specifically when the products or data will be turned over. Coordination of rules for handing off requires allowing enough lead time for doing the work as well as putting it back into production. Rules will be required for handling delays at your end as well as the service provider's end.

   - Break down accountability. Make sure each individual understands what he or she is accountable for doing or producing.

   - Define control mechanisms.

   - Document scheduling and commitment procedures.

2. Communicate the plan to your staff. Make sure that everyone understands what is intended before meeting with the service provider. This will prevent misinterpretations about the service provider's role, enabling staff to modify expectations if necessary.

3. Work up procedures with the service provider. Develop communications, performance tracking, and escalation processes.

4. Reinforce "ownership" of the work and the process. Review the actual work procedures to make sure that accountability is clearly understood by both your company and the service provider.

5. Assign knowledgeable staff to assist the service provider.
   There is a tendency in large and small organizations to delegate coordination with service companies to the least-busy
   members of the staff, who may also be those with the least
   knowledge or the lowest motivation. Don't pay a lot of
   money to a company only to have them fail for lack of
   knowledge.

Once last piece of advice. If you are new to the outsourcing
arena and need assistance, don't be afraid to hire a firm to broker the
relationship development activities.

Epilogue

For too many years, people have refused to listen to the boy who cried wolf. Now the wolf is upon us, and some wonder if it's too late to react. That's why it's so important to recognize that the role of the Year 2000 leader is not to make the problem go away, but to bring the objectives into alignment with the art of the possible.

Where to from here? Your curative efforts will buy you much—besides survival. You have no choice but to do this work, but that shouldn't blind you to what you will gain:

- *For the first time, we will have a comprehensive overview of the entire computing resource that drives and supports our organizations.* So armed, we can finally understand exactly how much and in what ways the organization depends on technology. This might convince us to stop viewing technology as an overhead expense and start treating it as a capital investment—more important and more strategic than the bricks and mortar.
- *Done properly, this massive overhaul of our systems will be a scaled-up spring cleaning.* We'll emerge knowing not just where every-thing is but also what value we place on specific systems. Many

organizations have entered into arduous business process
reengineering projects to learn exactly this. There is immense
value in an organizational overview that allows us to sit back
and contemplate what we have created during the past 35
years of computing.

• *Automating can be worth it!* You will acquire productivity tools
and impose rigor on your process, thereby reducing costs that
you have borne for years. We're not talking about economic
burdens alone, but also cultural ones that made it necessary for
you to reward performance on the basis of experience instead
of contribution.

• *We have an opportunity to become wiser and more efficient in our use
of technology.* Few people answer affirmatively when asked if
they were the best they could be. Now the job is to identify
what you did wrong and, perhaps more important, why you
did it that way. The answers, by helping you avoid the same old
mistakes, may direct you to a brighter future.

The Year 2000 problem is not about two missing digits, inadequate storage, or saving keystrokes. We believe it is about a failure in
communication between the technology experts and management
concerning the proper role of technology inside a business. It opens
questions that reach far beyond the scope of this book—questions
about the business process and even about human nature.

*Once the urgency of the problem was acknowledged in the late 1980s and
early 1990s, why didn't everyone move more rapidly to implement a fix?* The
Year 2000 problem was known well in advance of the current crisis.
No enterprise can claim they weren't warned or didn't have full dis-
closure of the consequences. Many in IT argue that they had no budget and no choices because they weren't calling the shots. If those
claims have validity, we are, in effect, admitting that we abdicated
responsibility.

*How did an industry, praised for its innovation and cleverness, drop the
ball so badly?* Many will reject this characterization outright. They will

try to point the finger at management, arguing that what was delivered to business was exactly the quality of software management was willing to pay for—no more, no less. Some have suggested that the aforementioned benefits should have been enough to convince management to act on the crisis. They might be right if not for one aspect of this project: the cost of failure. In the end, pointing fingers is useless. We should instead examine what went wrong and make sure we learn something from the $600 billion semester at the school of hard knocks.

Once we began to understand how the problem originated, why did we let ourselves continue to write systems destined to fail at a predetermined date? It's all too easy to allow the challenge of managing technological change to become an end in itself. Irrespective of its origins, the Year 2000 problem could not have persisted had IT not lost sight of why businesses invest in technology in the first place: to support the business.

Has management created a no-win dynamic whereby IT is responsible but not empowered? It is potentially more interesting to understand why IT wandered down the path of least resistance than to understand how the Year 2000 came to be. Since 1965, even novice programmers knew that two-digit years would not work in the Year 2000. Management heard and then ignored them. The programmers in turn accepted being ignored, opting to remain silent instead of rattling cages until someone listened.

Long after we've made our Year 2000 fixes it will behoove us to keep these questions open—indeed to keep our minds open—and to entertain a variety of answers. Computer technology represents a new way of life, and the problems it creates, however logical and predictable, will continue to surprise and challenge us.

The Year 2000 problem forces us to make hard decisions about what is essential for doing business day by day and what is not. Philosophical dimensions aside, however, the Year 2000 problem is not rocket science. It may be ugly and it may be unwieldy, but we have the technical know-how and the tools to lick it. What we need now is the necessary level of commitment.

You will, in the end, fix it to ensure the survival of your enterprise. Then, and only then, can you capitalize on the residual benefits—not only to pay back the cost of their acquisition, but to make it possible to look back on this crisis 20 years hence and reflect that the Year 2000 was the best thing that ever happened to the IT industry: It was the catalyst that turned us into professionals.

Peter de Jager
Richard Bergeon

Index